MINNEAPOLIS

MINNEAPOLIS

Barbara Flanagan

St. Martin's Press New York

To the dear man I met in St. Paul and married—
but only after he moved to Minneapolis.

ACKNOWLEDGEMENTS

May I say "thank you" again to those who egged me on, including:
*The late Frank P. Leslie, Minneapolis bibliophile and art connoisseur, who encouraged me to correspond with his friend, J. Paul Getty.
*My boss, Robert W. Smith, publisher of the *Minneapolis Star* and the *Minneapolis Tribune* and former *Star* editor.
May I also thank all of the VIPs who took time to talk to me about Minneapolis and especially:
*Senator Hubert H. Humphrey, former Mayor of Minneapolis and former Vice President of the United States.
*Maestro Eugene Ormandy of the Philadelphia Orchestra, former conductor of the Minnesota Orchestra.
Additional thanks must go to those who gave me so much help, including:
*Boris Sokoloff of the Philadelphia Orchestra.
*Dorothy Burke of the Minneapolis Public Library.
*Robert Lopez, chief librarian of the Minneapolis Star and Tribune Company.
As I write these acknowledgements, a 99-year-old Minneapolis grain and flour-milling firm is about to announce a gift to the city.
To observe its 100th year, the Peavey Company is giving a new downtown park-plaza to Minneapolis. Designed by M. Paul Friedberg & Associates, New York landscape and urban design firm, it will feature a large ornamental pool, terraces and fountain sculptures.
The Peavey park-plaza will adjoin the new Minneapolis concert hall and serve as a focal point in extending the Nicollet Mall from downtown to Loring Park at the edge of the business district.
This splendid civic gesture is an excellent example of what this book is all about. Thanks to Peavey and people like them, Minneapolis is looking forward to a great future.

October, 1973

MINNEAPOLIS

*Charlie Hoag, the Philadelphia schoolteacher
who named Minneapolis*

If you think about it, "Minneapolis" is a funny name for a place. Minneapolitans, the people who live there, never think about it. They like Minneapolis, both the name and the place. Most other people like Minneapolis too, once they know where to find it. Minneapolis (Mpls.) is in Minnesota (Mn.).

Minneapolis, the biggest city in Minnesota, has a population of 434,400. Directly across the Mississippi River is St. Paul with 309,980 residents, according to the 1970 census. The seven-county metropolitan area dominated by the Twin Cities had a population of 1,814,000 as of 1970, and is growing. The metropolitan area ranked fifteenth on the official census list of the nation's most populous urban areas. Minneapolis was thirty-second and St. Paul forty-sixth on the 1970 list of the fifty major cities. No other Minnesota cities made it.

Most people who consider themselves Minneapolitans or St. Paulites live in the suburbs and usually identify with one or the other of the Twins. The truly broad-minded, however, consider themselves to be Twin Citizens. In 1967 the Twin City area moved firmly toward metropolitan government by establishing the Metropolitan Council. Members represent Minneapolis in Hennepin County, St. Paul in Ramsey County and the surrounding suburban counties of Carver, Scott, Dakota, Washington and Anoka. The Council's role is to cope with problems that affect the total area, such as sewage disposal and rapid transit.

Minneapolis sits mostly on the west bank of the Mississippi river, east of St. Paul and about 425 miles downstream from the river's source in Itasca State Park. In the park you can jump the mighty Mississippi in one hop. In downtown Minneapolis it's a dangerous 600-foot swim from the west river bank to the east.

From Lake Itasca in the park, the Mississippi flows north for about fifty unnavigable miles to Bemidji, Minnesota, a dandy resort community that really enjoys its subzero winters. Bemidji, a summertime hay fever haven in the pine tree and lake country, is 226 miles north of Minneapolis by car. By river from Bemidji south to Minneapolis is a grueling 375 miles of paddling your own canoe. Nevertheless, modern-day *voyageurs* in canoes continue to make the trip for summertime adventure.

Minneapolis shouldn't be and rarely is confused with St. Paul, its fraternal and long-suffering Twin. St. Paul is southeast of downtown Minneapolis and across the Mississippi on the river's east bank.

Both cities are 350 miles by car or fifty minutes by air northwest of Chicago. Planes shuttle back and forth almost hourly all day long. On breakfast flights, commuters have to eat fast. New York is two and a half hours east of the Twin Cities by plane; San Francisco is three hours to the west. You get a snack only during the hour's flight to Kansas City, to the south. Dallas, Texas, takes two hours, time enough for a full-course meal.

What many people forget is that Canada is just across Minnesota's northern border. Winnipeg, Manitoba, is 426 miles by car from the Twin Cities or an hour by air. The scenery and greenery along the way are worth the motor trip.

The University of Minnesota, a city in itself with 40,000-plus enrollment, is in Minneapolis on the east bank. To further complicate matters, the University's "farm campus" or College of Agriculture is also on the east bank, but in a suburb of St. Paul known as Falcon Heights. In the last decade a part of the University—social sciences, business and fine arts—moved across the river to a new west bank campus, also in Minneapolis.

Today the Twin Cities get along better than ever before. They share the Minnesota Twins baseball team, an American League club; the Minnesota Vikings football team of the National Football Conference; and the Minnesota North Stars, a professional hockey team in the National Hockey League. All of the pros play home games in a suburb south of both Twin Cities—Bloomington, Minnesota (pop. 81,761). Picking the biggest suburb as the site for the stadium and ice center made sharing for the Twins a bit easier to take.

The need by the Vikings for a bigger stadium has sparked a new metropolitan hassle, however. A proposed domed stadium in downtown Minneapolis angered enough fans and scared so many Minneapolis taxpayers that it was rejected by voters. To date, the stadium and its location remains unsettled.

Another friendly hands-across-the-river gesture came in 1969 when the then sixty-eight-year-old Minneapolis Symphony Orchestra changed its name to the Minnesota Orchestra. Cynics said the only reason for the change was to pacify St. Paul residents on the orchestra's board of directors and to make it easier to raise funds in St. Paul. The official explanation is that the orchestra, founded in Minneapolis in 1903, serves and represents all of Minnesota today. The name change was designed to reflect its new role.

It is obvious now to most solid Twin Citizens that Minneapolis and St. Paul can work things out amicably. The Twins' next cooperative venture will be a metropolitan zoo. Its site in the suburb of Apple Valley is about seventeen miles south by freeway from the downtowns of both cities.

Since 1969, a freeway between the two business districts makes getting together even easier. The trip today is a quick twelve minutes by car. In older times the fastest link was by electric streetcar. The trolleys used to make the run in a rattling good half-hour, but they disappeared in 1954.

Before we start our tour of Minneapolis, I'll make a good Minneapolitan try at summing up St. Paul. St. Paul has been a commercial center and a river port since it was settled in 1838. Until 1971 when the paddle-wheeler, the Delta Queen, went temporarily out of service, passenger riverboats continued to dock there.

The Northern States Power Co. plaza at 5th St., and the Nicollet
Mall on a crowded, sunny Sunday in 1966 when the power firm staged
a free concert by the Minnesota Orchestra conducted by Stanislaw
Skrowaczewski. The picture shows Powers store facing Nicollet at 5th,
where it has always been, Penneys (which is a part of the old Syndicate
Block) and down 5th St. At the right rear are the columns of the former
Federal Reserve bank which stands at 5th and Marquette. These free
concerts are annual events.

Barges still keep the port of St. Paul busy. The hope is, however, that a new Delta Queen or two will come chuffing up the river someday soon. A riverboat at the St. Paul landing is historically fitting. St. Paul, a city of hills and valleys, is older and closer to its history than Minneapolis. St. Paul residents care more about traditional landmarks, and work at preserving them.

Don't misunderstand. There are no old-fashioned, nonprogressive fuddy-duddies in St. Paul, no matter what some Minneapolitans like to think. A love and a respect for the old hasn't prevented St. Paul from refurbishing its downtown business district. The boom is still going on.

In 1849 St. Paul became the capital of the Minnesota territory. It was incorporated as a city in 1854 and became the capital of Minnesota, the thirty-second state, in 1858. The state Capitol Building and all sorts of official state offices are there, including the Governor's mansion.

During the past fifty-seven years, the names of Minnesota governors have read like the roster for a Scandinavian lodge banquet. Olson and Johnson, Nelson, two Andersons and an Andersen have served as Governor, along with Burnquist, Christianson, Preus, Petersen, Benson, Thye, Youngdahl, Freeman, Rolvaag, and LeVander.

Currently, Wendell Anderson, a forty-year-old, curly-haired and handsome Swede, is Minnesota's thirty-third Governor. Anderson, a St. Paul lawyer and a Democrat, once skated on the U.S. Olympic hockey team. Oddly enough, only one of Minnesota's post-World War II Scandinavian governors spoke a Scandinavian language fluently. Anderson's immediate predecessor, Republican Harold LeVander, speaks Swedish so well that as Governor he often made speeches in it. When he did, there were enough Minnesota Scandinavians in the audience to understand him.

St. Paul is "home" to the Minnesota Archdiocese of the Roman Catholic Church and to a lot of people who once figured as characters in books by a St. Paul native, F. Scott Fitzgerald. Fitzgerald completed his first best-selling novel, *This Side of Para-*

Minnehaha Falls in winter.

(Left) The Guthrie Theater.

dise, in a room at the top of a town house on St. Paul's grand Summit Avenue. The house at 599 Summit is still a very good address in St. Paul. Zelda, Scott's wife and favorite heroine, lived in St. Paul briefly and didn't like it. Her opinion of Minneapolis was never recorded.

Another writer, Alvin Karpis, once Public Enemy Number One, called St. Paul "a crook's haven." In his biography, "The Alvin Karpis Story," published in 1971, he wrote, "Every criminal of any importance in the 1930's made his home in St. Paul. If you were looking for a guy you hadn't seen for a few months, you usually thought of two places: prison or St. Paul."

Of course St. Paul has changed its ways pertaining to criminals. And St. Paulites would like to forget the past, if only Minneapolitans would let them.

St. Paul has a thirty-nine-year-old civic opera company, a fine science museum, a splendid chamber orchestra, a growing art collection in the Minnesota Museum of Art, the excellent Minnesota State Historical Society museum, many elegant old homes and buildings, plus a zoo in Como Park, one of St. Paul's eleven major parks. Since 1882, a St. Paul institution known as the Schubert Club has brought top concert artists to the city.

Recently, a determined St. Paul woman, Mrs. John Musser, led a group of residents and city officials in a successful fight to save the city's magnificent old federal courthouse from destruction. It will now house cultural activities of the St. Paul Arts and Science Council.

The 3-M Company (Minnesota Mining & Manufacturing Co.) of Scotch Tape fame is based in St. Paul. So is its founder, William L. McKnight, retired board chairman of 3-M. McKnight, said a report by the U.S. Internal Revenue department in the 1960's, is Minnesota's richest man. His wealth at that time was estimated to be between 100 and 200 million dollars. His only child, Mrs. James H. Binger, lives on the Minneapolis side of

(Right) The new Minneapolis skyline looking across Loring Park lake with IDS Tower and Foshay Tower. May 1972.

the Mississippi in the silk-stocking suburb of Wayzata, twenty-five minutes west of downtown on Lake Minnetonka. Jim Binger is board chairman of Honeywell, a Minneapolis firm famous for thermostats in the White House and lots of computers everywhere around the world.

Lake Minnetonka, twelve miles long, with 110 miles of shoreline, may be the most famous of Minnesota's "10,000 Lakes." (At the last count there were approximately 23,000 lakes in the state.) In 1917 composer Thurlow Lieurance was inspired to write the popular tune, "By the Waters of Lake Minnetonka."

St. Paul boasts several fine colleges and two sitting U.S. Supreme Court Justices—Chief Justice Warren Burger and Associate Justice Harry Blackmun. Both are considered "St. Paul boys." Associate Justice William O. Douglas is also a Minnesotan. He is a native of the village of Maine, Minnesota, about 200 miles northwest of the Twin Cities in Otter Tail county.

One of the most famous nineteenth-century Minnesotans was James (Jim) J. Hill, a St. Paul resident who built the Great Northern railroad. He was known as "The Empire Builder." Hill's mansion at 240 Summit Avenue was designated as a National Historic Landmark by the National Park Service in 1961. It now houses offices of the Catholic Diocese of St. Paul. Hill's most famous monument, the 1881-vintage stone arch railroad bridge, spans the river in the middle of Minneapolis, a few hundred yards below St. Anthony Falls.

Fur trading, railroads, dry goods retailing, livestock and beer all helped build St. Paul. The German settlers made the beer. They and the Irish settlers bought and sold it. Today, St. Paul is a center for banking, trucking, manufacturing and electronics. The Germans continue to brew good beer. And the Irish still operate the saloons.

St. Paul's prominent philanthropists include the Hill family, McKnight, his colleague at 3-M, the late Archibald Bush, and a delightful octogenarian, I. A. O'Shaughnessy.

Ignatius Aloysius O'Shaughnessy, a millionaire oilman, has given generously to educational and civic institutions not only in

St. Paul, but throughout the area. The most recent of his gifts is O'Shaughnessy Hall, the new St. Paul hall for the Minnesota Orchestra.

The St. Paul Winter Carnival, an outdoor festival dating from 1886 and staged annually during the coldest week of winter brings out the hardiest spectators from both of the Twin Cities.

That should be enough about St. Paul in a book about Minneapolis, except for this: anybody coming to Minneapolis from the east—Milwaukee, Indianapolis or the megalopolis on the seashore side of the Hudson river—will hit St. Paul first.

Lakes are Minneapolis' most noticeable landmark from the air. The other, unfortunately, is blocks of unsightly parking lots. You've heard about those "wide open spaces" out West? They begin in downtown Minneapolis. Fortunately, city planners are aiming to someday put cars somewhere else.

Only two bridges among a dozen that cross the Mississippi in Minneapolis lead directly from St. Paul into town. On the Lake Street bridge, a sign in the middle marks the city lines.

On the west bank of the river, Minneapolis sprawls onto a windy, tree-shaded prairie dotted with twenty-three lakes. That is, twenty-three lakes INSIDE the city limits, plus 153 parks. To the south are more lakes and rich agricultural country. To the west are more lakes and wheat fields that cross borders into the Dakotas. And to the north are more lakes, a scenic resort country and the open pit iron mines.

Minneapolis' highest point, 981 feet above sea level, is in Waite Park in the northeast section of town. Its lowest is in Minnehaha Park on the river, 702 feet above sea level.

The largest park, Theodore Wirth, named after the city's most famous superintendent of parks, covers 143 acres. The total park system—land and water—adds up to 5,533.52 acres. That doesn't include another 608 acres at the city's International Airport.

Minneapolis' remarkable park system is only one reason why this city is so unique. Its setting on an undulating glacial plain between two rivers is another. The fifty-six-plus square miles that is Minneapolis proper is bordered on the south by the Minnesota

River. On the east is the Mississippi. That big stream, however, cuts the city in two as it flows from the north to meet the Minnesota.

Ask a long-time resident what he likes best about Minneapolis, though, and chances are, he will name the lakes and parks. A first-time visitor will agree. The visitor, however, usually also comments on Minneapolis' clean streets and fresh air.

What both forget to mention is the wind, which is ever-present. In winter the wind can cut you in two with cold. In summer our town is hot, but that same wind blows hard and cool. The constant wind has helped keep Minneapolis more or less free from fog, smog and air pollution. With growing motor traffic, however, air pollution is beginning to be an occasional problem. The wind may be Minneapolis' best hope in combating it.

There is nothing around big enough to stop the wind as it takes its sweeps and swipes at Minneapolis. That's why some of the taller buildings are structured to swing and sway with it. In 1972 the city's tallest modern skyscraper opened. The fifty-seven story building serves as the home office of Investors Diversified Services (IDS), a Minneapolis-based, multifaceted investment firm.

Throughout the year, the lakes are at the center of all outdoor recreation for Minneapolis and its suburbs. The city lakes belong to the taxpayers. They are open for public swimming, fishing, sailing and boating in summer. In winter, they stay open after a hard freeze for ice skating, hockey, ice boating, ice fishing and that rarified winter sport known to natives as skate sailing.

To skate sail, put on ice skates, get behind a big kite, and *go*.

There was a time around World War I when harness horses and cutters were raced on the ice of Lake of the Isles and Lake Harriet in winter. Today snowmobiles have taken over, but not inside the city limits. Young speed skaters are still assured of a good track for their events every year.

Minneapolitans, by the way, have a national reputation as good credit risks. It isn't unusual to find a boat AND a snowmobile sharing the same garage with a late-model car.

A Minneapolitan who owns a family sauna bath isn't considered to be among the superrich. Chances are, he thriftily built it himself. Minnesotans of Finnish ancestry have owned and used sauna baths for years. Most of them even stick to tradition and take a stark naked roll in the snow after their steaming.

In recent years, however, Minneapolis has become dotted with more sophisticated sauna bath parlors, whose bath attendants are usually beautiful girls. Their advertisements offer such inducements as "the loveliest girls at Barbie's Sauna" or "Oriental massage" at Kimiko's Sauna. Maggie's Midnight Sauna, Inc., uses the slogan, "Saunter in any time—we never close." The Soft Touch Sauna lets its name speak for itself.

Most saunas accept both men and women customers. But one suburban operation pulled a switch when it opened to women only and then staffed the place with male attendants.

Because St. Paul licensed saunas, they flourished in Minneapolis and were an attraction to both residents and visitors. Now, Minneapolis requires saunas to be licensed in an effort to make certain that services offered in the massage parlors are strictly legal.

Both youngsters and adults enjoy the outdoors in Minneapolis. Children grow up sailing small boats in regattas on the lakes or learning how to handle canoes. Old-timers while away many a winter afternoon crouching over holes in the ice waiting for fish to bite. Their fish-houses—boxy-looking structures resembling old-fashioned outhouses—may be one of Minnesota's major contributions to architectural history. Some of the more lavish fish-houses have been known to contain such amenities as electric heaters, well-stocked bars and TV sets.

The winter weather is more of a tease than a terror. Usually winter isn't as bad as claimed in the headlines of Florida newspapers. Temperatures in January, the coldest month, average 13.5 degrees above zero. Cold, true, but not Alaska.

Winter rarely keeps Minneapolitans indoors for very long. An ordinary, wind-whipped snowstorm doesn't stop anybody or anything in Minneapolis. The local feeling is that a good thick snow cleans the air and clears the nasal passages. Until the blizzard

Opening night at the Guthrie in 1963 when Sir Tyrone Guthrie staged "Hamlet" with, left to right holding hands at curtain call, Jessica Tandy as the Queen, George Grizzard as Hamlet and Lee Richardson as Hamlet's uncle.

(Left) The Nicollet Mall during one of the summer festival events. There are several art shows along it every year.

Dog-sledding on Lake Calhoun with a view of the still-abuilding IDS
Tower in January, 1972.

Vice President Hubert H. Humphrey (1968), presidential candidate, ex-senator and ex-mayor of Minneapolis, at Svenskarnas Dag (Swedish Day) festival in June with actress Ann-Margret, who was one of the super-star guests.

of March, 1966, closed down the town for a couple of days, the "big snow" best-remembered was the Armistice Day blizzard in November, 1941.

Cold winter nights in Minneapolis can be breath-taking. The wind loafs, the big and roomy night sky is packed with stars, and the quiet, even in the middle of the city, wraps itself around you.

In the suburbs, that quiet is often broken by caravans of snowmobiles. The noise from snowmobiles outrages some people and amuses others. Snowmobilers, zipped snugly into well-insulated snowmobile suits, love to get out and race around on top of the crisp snow.

Skiers, too, enjoy those brisk winter nights. Cross-country skiing and snowshoeing by torchlight in winter are two reasons why all Minneapolitans don't move south. Ski hills in the metropolitan area stay open late offering skiing "under the lights" for those who want to keep in trim during the work week. On weekends, skiers head north or west or east to bigger hills and mountains. Ski jumpers, however, stay home in the parks where jumps are available.

My point is that usually only the bears hibernate during a Minnesota winter. Everybody else just cat-naps, because the winter weather is too good to waste.

For some people the air is too fresh. They can't stand it for long. Usually, they take to wearing face masks over noses and mouths to make breathing easier.

Fur trading and fur ranching are historically big business in the Twin Cities area. The country's biggest fur auctions where pelts are sold to manufacturers have been held regularly in Minneapolis.

The manufacture of outdoor wearing apparel is another big local industry. Remember the "storm coat" that President Harry Truman wore in 1948? It was made in Minnesota. Clothes for skiers and snowmobile fans are also manufactured in the area.

What is most important is that Minneapolitans and all Twin Citizens have never stopped learning how to live with and enjoy their winter weather.

Today downtown Minneapolis has second-story pedestrian "skyways"—bridges connecting blocks in the loop of office buildings, hotels, parking ramps and retail stores. Shops, offices and restaurants open off the skyway system. Architect Philip Johnson of New York has called the all-weather links a modern version of the famed Ponte Vecchio in Florence, and "as unique to Minneapolis as are the canals and bridges of Venice."

In the design by Johnson and Baker Associates, Inc., of Minneapolis, for the block-wide IDS Center—dominated by the fifty-seven story skyscraper—four more pedestrian skyways join the system. During the next ten to fifteen years, city planners will expand the skyways to a total of sixty-four, linking buildings in fifty-four blocks of the downtown district. St. Paul is also adding a similar skyway plan to its downtown area.

At present over 25,000 people work in the skyway-linked buildings in Minneapolis, and have their own weekly newspaper, the *Skyway News*.

In the skyways it is always summertime, so who worries about the winter in Minneapolis? To live with it on bad days isn't exactly to love it, but Minneapolis residents know that winter is what makes their unique city even more so.

Summer of course is sensational. Usually it is naturally air-cooled and slightly silly. During the summer in Minneapolis, people who live in houses overlooking city or suburban lakes all winter go "to the lakes." They leave their city homes and head north (or south, east or west) to cottages on other lakes. Fortunately, everybody doesn't go to the lakes, and those who do, don't all go at the same time. Enough stay around town for the city's summer festival, the Minneapolis Aquatennial.

The name "Aquatennial" was coined by Rudolph Willer, an insurance adjuster and labor union executive. It won him a fifty-dollar prize in 1940. (In the thrifty Minneapolis tradition, Willer used the prize money to pay his dental bill.)

The Aquatennial centers on lake and water events, but it draws the biggest crowds to its parades, one under the sun and another by torchlight. Parade spectators come from miles around. So do parade participants. The Aquatennial parades, as well as the parks, lakes and picnic grounds in town, are open to the public.

The national boom in bicycle riding was forecast several years ago by the Minneapolis park commissioners when they voted to close city parkways to bike traffic only on Sundays from May through October. Bike paths that once were standard on city lakeshores were rebuilt to accommodate cycling crowds.

Minneapolis natives have been described in the past as "stolid" and "phlegmatic" by people who have never seen them at a hockey game. The natives also can and do get emotional over the parks and lakes. To tamper too much with Mother Nature can raise a public howl of protest.

Our city lakes have delighted all sorts of diverse types, among them naturalist Henry David Thoreau and strip-teaser Gypsy Rose Lee.

Thoreau came to Minneapolis for his health in 1861, the year before he died. He wrote of his joy in poking about the almost four miles of shoreline along Lake Calhoun, seeking birds, beasts and budding flora.

In his journal Thoreau recorded that he first saw the *geomys bursarius* near Lake Calhoun. You can see the *geomys bursarius* today on lake shores and lawns. Minnesotans know it as the gopher. They adopted it as the official state animal. University of Minnesota sports teams are always known as "the golden gophers."

Gypsy Rose Lee remembered Lake Calhoun and Lake Harriet from her childhood days of touring in vaudeville. She once told a newspaper reporter about the time she had to take an exam in order to graduate from elementary school. The only school giving the test at the time was in Hopkins, a Minneapolis suburb known to natives as "the raspberry capital of the world." It is an apt slogan. Hopkins grows great raspberries. "For three glorious days," Miss Lee recalled, "I climbed aboard a Como-Hopkins streetcar and had a wonderful ride all by myself around the lakes to and from school."

You too can take that same ride today by car, bike or bus. And thanks to the Minnesota Transportation Museum, Inc. (MTM), you can travel part of the way by streetcar. MTM members own a 1908 streetcar affectionately known as "old 1300," and they have rebuilt tracks between Lake Calhoun and Lake Harriet on the old streetcar right-of-way. During the summer months passengers can take a joy ride on the trolley between the two lakes.

The sight that draws most tourists and local residents throughout the year is Minnehaha Falls. After a soaking wet spring, the falls are at their best. Water flushes out of Lake Minnetonka, races along Minnehaha Creek through suburbs and city some twenty miles to Minnehaha State Park, overlooking the Mississippi. There the water drops over a cliff and falls fifty-three feet into a foaming pool. From the pool, the water slides down the bank to the river. In winter the falls freeze into enormous icicles. Henry Wadsworth Longfellow, who never actually saw the falls, described them quite lyrically in his poem, "The Song of Hiawatha."

Just above the falls in the park is a sculpture of Hiawatha, the young Sioux hero. He is portrayed carrying Minnehaha, the Indian maiden he loved, across the creek. It is a charming landmark, paid for by the pennies of schoolchildren.

Minneapolis also remembered Longfellow, Hiawatha, Minnehaha, and Hiawatha's grandmother, Nokomis, with street names. Nokomis also gave her name to a city lake.

In the city, Minnehaha Creek is bordered by pleasant homes and a tree-shaded boulevard, Minnehaha Parkway. Rubber-rafting down Minnehaha Creek is another typical summertime adventure for Minneapolitans of all ages.

The 160-acre Minnehaha Park is a great place for picnics. Organizations dominated by Swedes, Norwegians, Danes or Germans all stage big celebrations there every year. The Irish usually picnic in St. Paul.

It should be noted though that Minneapolis does have enough Irishmen (and their friends, the Poles, Italians, and Yugoslavs) to form a Minneapolis St. Patrick's Day association. The group sponsors a parade on March 17 to rival a similar march across the river in St. Paul. In Minneapolis, of course, the Scandinavians march right along with the Irish.

Swedes claim the biggest crowd at their annual *Svenskarnas*

Dag (Swedish Day) picnic every June. Usually about 20,000 Swedish-speaking, *lutfisk*-loving Swedes attend. That doesn't count the politicians who wouldn't miss it. No other *Svenskarnas Dag* is as big, except the one held in Sweden. The event, along with the Norwegian *Syttende Mai* (Independence Day), the German *Volkfest* and the Danish Day of the Danes, is typical of folksy Minneapolis.

The Wasps of New England got to town first and named it, but the Scandinavians and Germans put it together. Today residents of more than thirty nationalities give Minneapolis an international and very hospitable flavor.

Minneapolis is the chief retail center in the Upper Midwest, drawing shoppers from South Dakota and North Dakota to the west, Iowa to the south, plus Canada and western Wisconsin. It is also the cultural and entertainment hub of the area because of its major league sports and cultural attractions.

Timber was a big industry in Minneapolis until 1899. It didn't last—except on a smaller scale—but milling, Minneapolis' other historic big industry, has. The five largest milling firms in the world are based in Minneapolis, and food processing is big business.

Electronics, precision instruments, heavy machinery (including farm machinery), hearing aids, apparel, transportation equipment and computers are made in Minneapolis. Minneapolis is big in banking and is the site of the Ninth District, U.S. Federal Reserve bank. The Minneapolis Grain Exchange is the center of the largest cash grain market in the world.

Since 1945, four of the five men who have served as mayor—including former Vice President and now Senator Hubert H. Humphrey—could claim Scandinavian ancestors.

The present mayor, Charles Stenvig, is mostly Norwegian, but he probably won office because he ran as an independent candidate on a "law and order" platform. Stenvig, a former police detective, is a good-looking man in his early forties with a youthful face under a thatch of prematurely white hair. He has a shy smile, a sly sense of humor and a "just plain folks" attitude that keeps an adoring majority in his corner. The mayor doesn't work at being colorful, but he can swing out in a rhythmic "lindy hop" on social occasions or sit in with the band on drums. For some years, he played drums in the Minneapolis Police Band.

*　*　*

Charley Hoag didn't think Minneapolis was such a funny name. He coined it.

Hoag, a proper Philadelphia schoolteacher, took a scholar's approach to naming the clearing on the west bank of the Mississippi River, where he had settled in 1850. To the Greek word for city, *polis*, Hoag hitched up the Sioux (or Dakota) word for water, *minne*. He spelled it "Minnehapolis" with the "h" (for Hoag?) silent.

Hoag not only named Minneapolis, but he guaranteed the use of the name with a sly letter to the editor of the St. Anthony *Express*. When the committee to name the new place gathered at John Stevens' small house in November of 1852, Hoag was ready for them.

Several names had already been suggested. There were "Lowell" (the Wasps of New England arrived early) "Brooklyn" (there's a Brooklyn fan in every crowd) and "All Saints."

A letter sent to the St. Anthony *Express* signed "Minnehapolis," but attributed to Hoag, read in part: "The miserable misnomer, All Saints, is a name that is applicable to no more than two persons in the vicinity of the falls, and of doubtful application even to them."

Editor George D. Bowman agreed and wrote an editorial favoring Minneapolis. That did it, and the city of waters it became.

Hoag thought the name to be both poetic and proper, for the Indians were there first. The Sioux and later the Chippewa claimed Minneapolis. They fought over it often, even after the white settlers arrived and began to push the Indian tribes west and north and onto reservation lands.

For 100 years the Indian was faceless and forgotten in Min-

View of downtown skyline looking from the east bank (or St. Anthony Village side of the river, originally) across the 3rd Ave. bridge.

The towers, left to right are:

Clock tower is the Minneapolis city hall-Hennepin county courthouse, vintage 1898;

Building with "crown" is Northwestern Bell Telephone Co.

Next, with TV antenna, is 1929 Foshay Tower, a replica of the Washington monument;

Square glass building is First National Bank of Minneapolis.

Then, the mighty IDS Tower.

Then jump to the odd-looking and lower rectangular-looking structure still going up—that's the new Federal Reserve bank and the first building to be constructed a la the Golden Gate bridge.

And finally, the two buildings at far right are the Towers apartments in the old Bridge Square-Gateway area.

(Photo: Minneapolis Downtown Council)

(Right) Another Downtown Council shot of the Foshay and IDS Towers.

(Photo: Minneapolis Downtown Council)

neapolis. Only in the late 1960's did a new generation of Indians begin to speak up for their people. Today they are a visible and vocal part of the Minneapolis cityscape, involved civically and politically in what can truly be called their "own home town."

It was with the Sioux that young Lieutenant Zebulon Pike of the U.S. Army had to deal when he came into the Minnesota wilderness in 1805. Pike was sent by the government to "make peace" with the Sioux and the Chippewa who shared the new and unknown United States territory.

His other mission was to seek out sites for new military posts. The "enemy" then was the British, whose troops in nearby Canada still posed a threat to the new nation. Pike selected a site on the bluff 110 feet above a place where the Minnesota river meets the Mississippi.

The Sioux were willing to sell land. Pike's treaty gave the Indians $200, sixty gallons of liquor and a pledge for $2,000. It was not a very good deal for the Indians because the government "forgot" that it owed the Sioux $2,000. The debt wasn't paid until fourteen years later.

Pike, who is known to schoolchildren as the discoverer of a mountain peak in Colorado, was not around to remind Uncle Sam of the oversight. He died as an Army general in the War of 1812. In Minnesota, Pike's name was given to an island at the juncture of the two rivers where he made that first real estate deal with the Sioux.

The land Pike bought extended nine miles north from the river junction and included St. Anthony Falls, the water power that would help to build the city of Minneapolis.

North of the falls, the Indian lands of lakes and forests stretched hundreds of miles to the Canadian border. The only white men who knew that country were French fur traders, the fabled *voyageurs*.

One wonders today why the Indians allowed the white men

(Left) Sailboats on Lake Calhoun. A Greater Minneapolis Chamber of Commerce picture.

(Greater Minneapolis Chamber of Commerce photo)

to move so close to the waterfall. That area was hallowed ground where, some said, spirits walked in the watery mist. Old-timers wrote in their journals of Indian religious rites they had observed being performed on Spirit Island, in the river just below the falls, and on the nearby west bank.

The sight of the falls was a religious experience to the first white Christian who saw it in July, 1680—Father Louis Hennepin, a Catholic priest of the Franciscan order. Hennepin, a Belgian, had come to Canada, then French territory, as a missionary in 1675. In 1680 he joined the French explorer Robert De LaSalle on a trek into the new western territory. In February of that year Hennepin and two companions left LaSalle's camp in Illinois to explore the upper Mississippi river. En route up river, they were captured by the Sioux and taken to the site of the future city of St. Paul. From there, the three white men were led on a hike overland to the big Sioux camp on Lake Mille Lacs, about sixty-five miles north of Minneapolis.

When the Sioux left on a buffalo hunt, so the story goes, Hennepin was set free. It was on his return trip down the Mississippi that he discovered the falls. Hennepin named the waterfall after St. Anthony of Padua, patron saint of his Franciscan province in France. History records that Hennepin stood on the east bank of the river to look at the waterfall. That site, a fraction of an acre, is known today as Lucy Wilder Morris Park. The Hennepin County Historical Society now owns the park. It is in a new St. Anthony historic area now in the planning stages. The hope of city planners is to refurbish Minneapolis's historic river front.

As a starter, the riverbank adjacent to Lucy Wilder Morris park has been turned into a park and christened Father Hennepin Bluffs. The work was done by teen-agers and paid for by public funds.

Hennepin's name was given to the county of which Minneapolis is the major city. Hennepin Avenue is one of the city's main streets. At the western end of the downtown Hennepin Avenue stands the Catholic Basilica of St. Mary, with its splendid Renaissance facade. In front of it is a bronze figure of Father Hennepin, which was a gift to Minneapolis in 1930 from the Knights of Columbus of Minnesota. The gift commemorated the 250th anniversary of Hennepin's discovery of the falls.

There are Belgians who continue to claim today that Hennepin, not LaSalle, first discovered the Mississippi river. Downtown Minneapolis has a street named for LaSalle, but it stretches only twelve blocks. Hennepin Avenue is some seventy blocks long. De LaSalle, a Catholic high school operated by the Christian Brothers, is also named for the explorer.

De LaSalle stands on Nicollet Island, another of Minneapolis' remarkable landmarks. For approximately seventy years, the island, smack in the middle of the Mississippi at the city's center, was a forgotten backwater hidden behind the industrial area that grew up around it.

Nicollet Island and Minneapolis' main shopping street, the Nicollet Mall, were named for a Frenchman who didn't show up in the area until 1836. No one knows how much time Joseph N. Nicollet, a French-born astronomer and civil engineer, spent on the island. He was employed by the U.S. Government when he first came up the Mississippi to Fort Snelling. He planned to map the area, and during the four years he lived at the fort, he did so. In 1843, after his death, his map, the first authoritative map of Minnesota, was published.

Years before Nicollet arrived there, Fort Snelling was not only the "citadel on the Northwest frontier," but a bustling crossroads in the new wilderness. It was often home to many distinguished and intrepid early travelers.

The first of these travelers was Major Stephen H. Long, an Army engineer, who arrived at the bluffs overlooking the river junction in 1817. His mission was to take a second look at the site that Zebulon Pike had selected twelve years before. Long liked the site, and a temporary fort was established. Long, by the way, was also responsible for naming Minneapolis' Lake Calhoun after John C. Calhoun, Secretary of War in the Cabinet of President James Monroe.

The first commandant of the temporary fort, Lieutenant Colonel Henry Leavenworth, took charge in 1819 of what was then known as Fort St. Anthony. Of the year that Leavenworth spent there, at least one memento remains: Lake Harriet, which was named after his wife.

In 1820 Leavenworth was replaced by Colonel Josiah Snelling of Boston. It was Snelling who designed and built the fort of creamy Minnesota limestone during the years from 1820 to 1827. In 1824 General Winfield Scott, after an inspection tour of Snelling's still uncompleted limestone bastion, recommended that Fort St. Anthony be renamed Fort Snelling.

Today Fort Snelling is one of Minneapolis' and the nation's major historic sites. It has been restored by the Minnesota Historical Society, which saved it from destruction by freeway planners, and it is open to tourists from May through October.

Explorers, artists, engineers, writers, adventurers and such distinguished visitors as the widow of Alexander Hamilton made the then-fashionable, but somewhat foolhardy trip up the Mississippi to Fort Snelling. Artist George Catlin, who came to the Fort in 1835 to paint the Indians and the surrounding scenery, returned to "civilization" raving about Fort Snelling as a glorious vacation spot. The trip became so popular that the St. Louis Hotel was built near the fort and served tourists willing to brave the journey. Another well-known nineteenth-century American artist, Seth Eastman, is a part of Fort Snelling's history. He was fort commandant in the 1840's. Another famous commanding officer was President Zachary Taylor, who did his tour of duty there in 1828.

Among the explorer-adventurers, some of them dedicated scientists, such as Nicollet, were Giacomo Beltrami, a young Italian nobleman; Lewis Cass, Governor of Michigan territory, and Henry R. Schoolcraft, a young mineralogist. All three men sought

A view through the columns of the Northwestern National Life Insurance Co., building by Yamaski toward the skyline and up the Nicollet Mall.

The office of John S. Pillsbury, Jr., board chairman of Northwestern National Life Insurance Co., and the man who had the courage to build first in the urban renewal area downtown.

(Right) The late Sir Tyrone (Tony) Guthrie—his 6 foot, 7 inch head rearing above an intermission crowd—at the Guthrie Theater. Opening night, 1963.

the source of the Mississippi; Schoolcraft, on his second trip in 1832, finally discovered it in the lake he named Itasca.

There were others who stayed longer to work in the new land. The Pond brothers, Samuel and Gideon of Connecticut, came as missionaries to the Indians in 1834. Their cabin above the east shore of Lake Calhoun was the first house in what is now Minneapolis. A boulder bearing a bronze plaque marks the site today.

At Lake Calhoun the Sioux ruled by Chief Cloudman were being taught farming under an experimental program designed by Major Lawrence Taliaferro, Indian agent at the fort. The Pond brothers helped with that project, plotted the area and named their township Eatonville after John H. Eaton, Secretary of War under President Andrew Jackson.

Taliaferro, during his years at the fort from 1820 until 1839, worked hard to keep peace between the Sioux and the Chippewa. He also has gone down in history as a man who tried to protect the Indians from exploitation by white men.

Although many treaties were signed between the two Indian nations over the years, the Sioux in 1851 still camped on the west bank of the river above St. Anthony Falls. Colonel John H. Stevens, resident in the first house in what is now downtown Minneapolis, recalled in his memoirs that Indians of different tribes roamed his land in 1850-51. The Sioux camp was no more than three blocks from Stevens's cottage. It stood where the Burlington Northern Railroad depot is today.

Stevens noted that the Indians usually respected the private property of whites living outside Indian lands. The Indians, he reported, would occasionally take property and livestock from missionaries living on Indian lands, however. He indicated that

(Left above) Swedish folk-dancers on the green in Minnehaha Park for Svenskarnas Dag.

(Left below) Lovers beside Lake of the Isles—which is surrounded by one of the city's loveliest residential districts, the Kenwood-Lowry Hill area—in summer.

white settlers and Indians usually got along, but Indians and Indians didn't.

In 1853 Sioux and Chippewa fought a battle in downtown St. Paul. Even at that time, it was a blooming community. That battle may have brought about the final push by the white government to rid the area of the "savages." In 1854 the Sioux were officially moved from their villages in the Twin Cities area to a new land in western Minnesota. The land west of the Mississippi, all of Minneapolis and its suburbs, was opened to white settlers in 1851. The white man moved in fast. The Sioux and then the Chippewa continued to be moved west and north, eventually to be legally "penned up" on reservation lands they still hold today.

Stevens, who arrived at the falls in 1849, was married and settled on the river's west bank by 1851. He came to work for the fort's sutler, Franklin Steele. Steele, by the way, was probably Minneapolis' first real estate speculator. Starting as the storekeeper at the fort, he eventually owned it. From 1857, when the government sold it to him, until 1861, Steele operated a sheep farm at the old outpost. In 1861 the fort was reactivated and remained a military post until 1946.

Steele amassed two fortunes during his forty-odd years in Minneapolis. He also helped build the University of Minnesota and served as chairman of its first board of regents. In later life he moved to Washington, D.C., but ironically his death came while he was in Minneapolis on business. History books state that in 1880 Steele was "stricken while driving down Hennepin Avenue with his old friend, Captain John Tapper, the man who ran the first ferryboat across the Mississippi at Minneapolis."

The city named a park after him, as they did for many early settlers, including Colonel Stevens, but not including Charley Hoag.

There is room for a Hoag Square right now at 5th Street and Hennepin Avenue in downtown Minneapolis. That corner is where Hoag first farmed in the new city. At the end of the nineteenth century and through forty years of the twentieth, on Hoag's first farm site stood the elegant West Hotel, which old-timers say reeked with class. The hotel was razed in 1940, and today Hoag's farm is a dirty parking lot.

In 1872, Minneapolis annexed St. Anthony on the east bank. Men with New England roots named Eastman, Bell, Gale, Chute, Morrison, King and Pillsbury moved in to build the new city. The early movers and shakers also included men named Washburn, Phelps, Lowry, Peavey, Bull, Welles, Kingman, Bovey and Crosby. Donaldson and Loring, Brackett and Salisbury, Heffelfinger and Wells, Atwater and Walker, Fruen and Gluek were involved too.

Young Eastmans today are as interested in Nicollet Island as a restoration project as their ancestors John and W. W. Eastman were. John, in the 1850's, built the first flour mill at St. Anthony Falls. W.W., who joined him in business, was the developer of Nicollet Island. It was a pleasant residential district from the 1860's until World War I.

The Walker family, Minneapolis pioneers in culture and social welfare institutions, continue to care. The new Walker Art Center is the result of a collection lumberman Thomas Barlow Walker began in 1874. The Walker family also gave the land for the Guthrie theater and started the institution that is now the Walker Methodist Residence for the Aged.

Dorilus Morrison was Minneapolis's first mayor. His son, Clinton, gave the land where the Minneapolis Institute of Arts now stands. Dorilus' grandson, also Clinton, a Minneapolis bank executive, headed the board of trustees of the museum at the kickoff of that organization's drive to raise funds for the new addition designed by architect Kenzo Tange of Japan.

Internationally, the most instantly-recognized Minneapolis name belongs to the Pillsbury family, thanks to a Minnesota governor's nephew's flour mill. The lively Pillsbury family today is an excellent example of a tradition of civic spirit that dates back more than 120 years.

The Pillsburys came from New Hampshire. John Sargent Pillsbury arrived first in June of 1855, opened a hardware store and lost his shirt—or at least a couple of shirt-sleeves. He paid off his debts and by 1875 had a flourishing wholesale hardware business. By that time he was already involved in politics and with the young state university. It was Pillsbury who, as a state senator, offered the bill putting the floundering university under the direction of a board of regents. He was appointed a regent in 1863 and served until his death in 1901.

Pillsbury continued to pursue politics with success. He was elected Governor of Minnesota in 1875 and re-elected in 1877 and 1879. In 1881 he turned down the opportunity for a fourth term.

In 1869 Pillsbury invited his nephew, Charles A. Pillsbury, to join him in Minnesota. Young Charlie was to become the family flour miller, founding the firm Charles A. Pillsbury & Co., in 1870. Charlie's Uncle John and his father, George A. Pillsbury, were partners.

George A., the governor's brother and the miller's father, didn't move to Minneapolis right away. In Concord, New Hampshire, he worked successfully as purchasing agent for a railroad for some twenty-seven years. He dabbled in city politics, served in the New Hampshire legislature, was involved in construction and helped found the First National Bank of Concord in 1864. When he came to Minneapolis in 1878 at the age of sixty-two, George A. Pillsbury left his job as bank president behind. He also left behind a long civic career in Concord and the mayor's office, a post to which he was elected in 1876.

By 1884 George A. Pillsbury was the elected mayor of Minneapolis, at age sixty-eight. One of his official acts as mayor was to create the city "patrol limits," an area of the city in which all licensed liquor establishments remain to this day. Pillsbury's purpose was to make it easy for the foot patrolman of that era to police bars and saloons. Over the years, succeeding Minneapolis politicos have attempted to expand or abolish the "patrol limits." To date, they have had no success.

George A. lived and died working to better Minneapolis. He died in 1898 at home on the site of the present Leamington Hotel. His nephew, the governor's son, was Alfred F. Pillsbury, perhaps the family's first knowledgeable art connoisseur and collector of Chinese bronzes. He served on the board of the milling firm his cousin headed, and he also owned a water power company. His collection and the Minneapolis Institute of Arts to which he left it were his major interests, however.

Richard Pillsbury Gale, Alfred's nephew, owns a collection of seventeenth-century Japanese paintings that is world-famous among art experts. Gale also shares the Pillsbury family's love for public service and was a Republican congressman from Minnesota in the U.S. House of Representatives.

Charlie Pillsbury—remember him?—the miller, had twin sons. They were named John Sargent Pillsbury and Charles Stinson Pillsbury. Both plunged into the milling business, as did some of their sons.

Philip W. Pillsbury, Charles Stinson's son, is honorary board chairman of the family company. That post was held by his uncle, John Sargent Pillsbury, until his death in 1968 at the age of 89.

During the years he was chief executive of the firm, Philip became expert at pancake-flipping and often made them in the test kitchens for visiting VIPs and members of the press. A bon vivant who, like his Uncle John, always wears a flower in his lapel, Philip is honorary consul general for France in the Upper Midwest area. In the family tradition, he has been active in affairs of the city's major cultural, educational and political organizations, as well as those of his school, Yale University.

His sister, Mary Pillsbury (Mrs. Oswald Bates) Lord is a former delegate to the United Nations, a writer and world traveler. One of Philip's sons is in the United States diplomatic corps. The other, an actor-writer-director, once operated a youth center in Paris.

Philip's cousins, children of John Sargent Pillsbury, include John S. Pillsbury Jr., chairman of the board of Northwestern National Life Insurance Co.

John S., Jr., a Yale graduate with a law degree from Minnesota, where his father was a proud alumnus, followed in the footsteps of the first Governor Pillsbury, his great-great-uncle, and ran for

The dirt road is Calhoun boulevard about 1900.

(Library of Congress)

(Right) American Indians seated beside Minnehaha Falls—about 1870.

that office in 1968. He failed to win the Republican nomination. His younger brother, George A., is serving his second term as a Minnesota State Senator.

George A. stayed with the milling firm until 1970. He resigned as a vice-president to devote his time to family affairs, civic activities and politics.

At the present time, there are no young Pillsburys growing up in the milling firm—a first in the firm's long and successful history. The sons of John S. Jr. and George A. may end up in politics, however.

To date, the family has produced one militant liberal, Charles A. Pillsbury, son of George A., the state senator. Young Pillsbury, also a Yale man, is founder of the Council for Corporate Review. It was formed to give peace-loving stockholders of Honeywell, the Minneapolis-based computer firm, a voice at the annual meeting in 1970, in an attempt to force Honeywell to stop making anti-personnel fragmentation bombs. The group, led by Pillsbury, made headlines, but the issue was never put to a vote.

More radical members brought revolutionary Jerry Rubin to town to help create a fuss. The ruckus happened, but Rubin didn't show up. (He said later that he overslept at his Minneapolis hotel.) Young Pillsbury's arm of the organization has continued to protest to Honeywell in a positive and peaceful manner via petitions and telephone calls.

His grandson's role as an activist would have delighted the late John Sargent Pillsbury, Sr. He liked to see his children get involved, because he always was. "I like people and I hope they like me," he used to say. He did and they did.

Pillsbury was a Minneapolis enthusiast. Even winter didn't stop him. In his eighties, he still owned and wore an ankle-length raccoon coat to the office on brisker days. He had watched in his

(Left) The glen below Minnehaha Falls around the turn of the century when gentlemen went fishing in derby hats and morning coats.

(Library of Congress)

lifetime as his hometown was built up and torn down and then built up again. His enthusiasm for beauty on the cityscape was passed along to John Jr.

When Minneapolis' skid row went down in an urban redevelopment program fifteen years ago, it was John Jr.'s life insurance company that made one of the first moves to rebuild in the center. Northwestern National Life's home office, designed by architect Minoru Yamasaki, was voted by Minnesotans as the most beautiful building in the state. John Jr.'s vision and belief in downtown Minneapolis helped start a trend and another Minneapolis building boom—about the fifth since the town was started.

While the Pillsbury men were helping to make Minneapolis grow, the Pillsbury women—wives and daughters—were not lolling around at home.

Mrs. John S. Pillsbury Sr., matriarch of the family, is an octogenarian with an abundance of grace, beauty, wit and brains. Educated in St. Louis and Europe, and reared in St. Paul, Mrs. Pillsbury moved to Minneapolis when she was married. Since that day, she has never spiritually been "out of it." What's more, she continues to be totally involved in any job she undertakes and interested in everything her large family is doing.

One daughter-in-law, Mrs. George A. Pillsbury, is active in Republican politics. A daughter, Mrs. Thomas Crosby, is a trustee of the Minneapolis Society of Fine Arts. Another daughter-in-law, Mrs. John S. Jr., served on the board of the Kennedy Center for the Performing Arts in Washington. And a niece, the late Mrs. Philip W. Pillsbury, was national president of Planned Parenthood and an activist in many social welfare organizations.

As the century turned from the nineteenth to the twentieth, another family began a tradition of civic involvement in Minneapolis: the Daytons.

"The Dayton Boys," as they are affectionately known around town, are a remarkable quintet of brothers. These third-generation natives—brothers Donald, Bruce, Wallace, Kenneth and Douglas, and their cousin, George—built the retailing giant known as the Dayton-Hudson Corp. They have also been in the middle of Minneapolis' present renaissance that put the city in the number two spot in the national "quality of life" ratings.

When their grandfather, a Worthington, Minnesota banker and real estate man, opened a dry goods store on Nicollet Avenue at 7th Street in 1901, he didn't plan to make a career of it. He owned the corner and he didn't have a tenant. Even though the store site was considered to be a bit far uptown for shoppers in those days, he went ahead.

In 1969 Dayton's, one of the nation's successful family-owned department stores, bought the J. L. Hudson Co. of Detroit and merged the two to form the multifaceted retailing giant, the Dayton-Hudson Corp. Today, the family department store is only one of its subsidiaries. Dayton-Hudson also operates shopping centers, discount stores, fine jewelry shops, a bookstore chain and other retail outlets from coast to coast.

Donald C. Dayton, oldest brother, headed the store until he retired to devote more time to civic activities. It was Donald who led the crusade to change old Nicollet Avenue into the new Nicollet Mall, a shopping haven downtown. Donald also took on the chairmanship of the National Alliance of Businessmen, an organization dedicated to finding employment for minority citizens. Interest in metropolitan government led him to an appointment to the Metropolitan Council.

Bruce B. Dayton, an art collector and patron, is chairman of the board of Dayton-Hudson. His interest in art inspired him to commission sculptor Alexander Calder to create a stabile for the city as a gift from Daytons. Originally, the stabile was on the Nicollet Mall in front of the store. It was moved to a site in front of the Walker Art Center to make room for another skyway bridge. Bruce is former chairman of the Minneapolis Society of Fine Arts, governing body of the Minneapolis Institute of Arts, Minneapolis College of Art and Design and the Children's Theatre at the Institute.

Wallace C., the third brother, resigned from the family firm a few years back to devote himself to conservation work and to such service organizations as the YMCA. He still serves as a member of the board of directors, however.

Kenneth N., president of Dayton-Hudson, is the family symphony orchestra buff. He is former president of the Minnesota Orchestral Association, governing body of the Minnesota Orchestra. In 1971 he was named to the twenty-six-man board of the National Council for the Arts.

Douglas J. Dayton, youngest of the five, resigned as senior vice-president of the corporation last year after seven years spent designing, launching and building the company's successful Target discount stores. At the time, he said he found top-level staff work too confining and unexciting and he wanted to find a more stimulating career course.

He took on the chairmanship of the Loaned Executive Action Program (LEAP) for Governor Wendell Anderson. The program used executives on loan from their companies to work on management problems in state government. He also headed the YMCA's fund-raising drive.

Douglas is now chairman of the board of Dade, Inc., a company he organized. It is designed to offer a package of capital and management to small firms. He also remains a member of the Dayton-Hudson board.

Cousin George was involved in family retailing and with the Greater Minneapolis Chamber of Commerce for years. He now heads the George Dayton Foundation, which sponsors ecumenical conferences for businessmen and clergy.

The firm contributes five per cent of its taxable income annually to charity or, as its report on corporate contributions reads, "for the improvement of the communities of which it is a part." In 1972, the corporation and the Dayton Hudson Foundation gave a total of $1,637,000. Most of it goes to support the arts or to develop social-action projects. Among the more unusual causes

(Right) Here's a 1902 View of Minnehaha Falls.

Looking up Nicollet Ave., in 1886 from the 3rd St. corner. The gas chandelier decor was installed for some exposition.

Again, around 1886, standing about in Bridge Square and looking up
Nicollet Ave., on the left and Hennepin Ave. on the right. With a very
wide angle lens, this could still be shot by standing on Pillsbury's
Northwestern Life Insurance lawn and pointing the camera toward the
Mall and the Nicollet hotel.

supported was the funding of a course on social change for Minneapolis police. Money has also been donated to a group seeking to build a bicycle path across a portion of Minnesota.

The Daytons realized early that if, as a corporation, they were to get involved on the urban scene, they should have experts representing them. The executive in charge of civic activities—who also heads the Foundation—is a former city manager.

Dayton wives, in typical Minneapolis style, are also totally involved with the city. Mrs. Donald Dayton was the first woman elected to the United Fund board in the post-World War II era. Mrs. Wallace Dayton has presided over the Minneapolis YWCA board and Mrs. Kenneth Dayton is the first woman to serve as president of the board of Walker Art Center.

The Dayton brothers grew up learning to be active in Minneapolis because their parents, the late Mr. and Mrs. George Nelson Dayton, lived by such standards. Today, a fourth generation of Daytons is in the retailing business and in Minneapolis civic life—and a fifth generation is coming along.

Today, too, the sons and grandsons of the Scandinavian immigrants who followed the Wasps to Minneapolis, are active workers on the civic scene: Curtis L. Carlson, hotel and trading stamp millionaire; H.P. Skoglund, insurance executive; Roy Larsen, Russell Johnson, Lloyd Swanson and Harold Greenwood, savings and loan company leaders; Lester Malkerson, automobile executive; Donald Knutson, builder; Walter Nelson, real estate executive; and Carl Granrud, who built Lutheran Brotherhood, an insurance firm for Lutherans; and Russell Lund, who heads a local grocery chain bearing his name.

Minneapolis' leading individual philanthropist, Jay Phillips, is Jewish, but his giving has been ecumenical and covers all bases: cultural, educational, religious, medical and social welfare. His business interests embrace everything from airlines to wholesale liquor.

Phillips' son, Morton, whose wife is Abby Van Buren, the nationally-syndicated advice columnist, is as active as his father. Morton, however, puts special emphasis on cultural organizations. He is also the first member of the Jewish faith to be elected to the board of the Minneapolis YMCA.

John Cowles, retired founder of the Minneapolis Star and Tribune Company, and his son, John Jr., chairman of the board, have also been leading givers to Minneapolis. John Jr., headed the campaign for $2.3 million in private funds to build the Tyrone Guthrie Theatre. Most of the money was raised in the Twin Cities.

* * *

Who else calls Minneapolis "home"?

There are twenty-six pages of Johnsons in the Minneapolis telephone book—more, it's claimed, than in any other city in the world. (And that's not counting Johnstons).

Only in Minneapolis do the Joneses try to keep up with the Johnsons—at least, numerically. In recent history, however, three Jones "boys" have made the name memorable.

There was Robert Jones, a top-hatted gentleman known as "Fish." Robert was Fish Jones from the day he opened a downtown fish market in 1876 until his death in 1930. He gained real fame with his private zoo. It was open to the public on his property near Minnehaha Park. His house, a smaller replica of Henry Wadsworth Longfellow's house in Cambridge, Massachusetts, became the Longfellow branch of the Minneapolis Public Library after his death. Today, while the city decides whether to preserve it or raze it, it's used as a warming-house for young ice skaters.

Herschel V. Jones was publisher of the former Minneapolis *Journal* and a knowing art collector. Minneapolis can thank him for the jewel of the painting collection at the Minneapolis Institute of Arts—Rembrandt's *Lucretia*. Jones discovered the then unknown painting and brought it back to hang in the Great Hall of his house on Park Avenue. It has belonged to Minneapolis ever since.

Today the best known of the Joneses is Will Jones, the anti-smoking gourmet and entertainment columnist of the Minneapolis *Tribune*. Where Will goes to dine and sip wine, crowds follow.

Outsiders should understand that Scandinavians in Minneapolis—Swedes, Norwegians, Danes, Icelanders and Finns—may fuss among themselves on occasion, but most of their problems are usually solved over a good cup of strong coffee.

Probably the most infamous resident of Minneapolis was Irish, not Scandinavian, but John Dillinger really didn't stay long enough to put down roots. In the 1930's, when he was the nation's Public Enemy Number One, Dillinger did set up housekeeping in a south Minneapolis apartment with the then-current love of his life, Evelyn Frechette.

Few Minneapolitans remember them today, but a retired grocer recalled for me that Dillinger and Miss Frechette were a quiet couple you wouldn't even notice. What made them memorable to the grocer is that in that Depression era, they always paid their grocery bill.

Few Minneapolis residents today realize that their town was the birthplace of a man who has been called "the world's richest"—J. Paul Getty, the oil billionaire. Getty, who now lives in the 450-year-old mansion, Sutton Place, outside of London, England, was born in a brownstone close to downtown Minneapolis on December 15, 1892. His father, George F. Getty, a successful Minneapolis lawyer, invested in some Oklahoma oil lands at the right time.

Getty last visited his old hometown in 1947. A few years after that, the late Bob Murphy, former Minneapolis *Star* columnist, interviewed him in England. The oil man had many vivid memories of his Minneapolis boyhood, recalling the apartment on Hennepin Avenue where he lived when he went to Emerson grammar school. Both the school and the apartment were close to Loring Park where Getty went ice skating and sliding in winter. Wesley Methodist Church, to which the Getty family belonged, is still standing. Unfortunately, Minneapolitans do not mark the haunts of famous natives with historical plaques. The fact that J. Paul Getty once slept on Hennepin Avenue might surprise some natives as well as tourists.

Getty recalled his excitement whenever the family took a buggy ride twenty miles out from town to Lake Minnetonka. The purpose of the jaunt usually was to view the grand tourist hotels. Those showplaces disappeared a long time ago. Getty referred to the hotels as "humdingers."

The late Frank P. Leslie, former board chairman of the John Leslie Paper Co. of Minneapolis, and the late Mrs. Leslie, often visited Getty in England. Mrs. Leslie, the former Ruth Hill, a member of the pioneering family that helped found Janney Semple Hill, a wholesale hardware firm, was Getty's schoolmate at Emerson grammar. Leslie recalled that Getty has often said that Ruth Hill Leslie was his first boyhood "crush." It was through the Leslies that Getty made his grandest gesture to Minneapolis. In 1967, Leslie carried a letter to Getty from trustees of the Minneapolis Society of Fine Arts. It asked for the loan of two of Getty's paintings: a self-portrait by Veronese and Raphael's painting of the Madonna of Loreto, a masterpiece Getty discovered, recognized and bought for only $195. Getty paid all the costs to ship the two pictures to the Minneapolis Institute of Arts. And although they went on exhibit during one of Minneapolis' coldest Januarys, 26,000 people trekked out to see them.

In 1972, thanks again to Leslie, Getty loaned a collection of his art to the Institute for a summer exhibit. It, too, attracted people—about 50,000—during its longer stand.

In a recent exchange of letters with Getty, I asked him if his interest in art collecting was influenced by his Minneapolis boyhood. I wondered if he had climbed to the top of the old public library where the Minneapolis School of Art once held classes. I also thought he might have peeked into the gallery that Thomas Barlow Walker, Minneapolis lumberman, opened to the public in his Hennepin Avenue home.

Getty replied that he was very fond of the old library and had been sorry to see it razed, because he had visited it often as a boy. "I don't recall wandering into Mr. T.B. Walker's house to see his pictures," Getty wrote, "although I knew who he was."

"I left Minneapolis in 1906 when I was thirteen. I don't believe I thought much about art until I was in my twenties."

Getty's best memories of his hometown are of winter when he dared to "hitch" his sled behind a streetcar for a thrilling free ride on the icy street to the top of Lowry Hill.

*   *   *

What of those famous Minneapolis Johnsons? Well, everywhere you go in town somebody named Johnson is doing a good job. It would take another book to write about all of them.

Among them is Andrew N. (for Nissen) Johnson, a distinguished Minneapolis lawyer who served many years as honorary Consul General of Denmark in the Upper Midwest area.

And Charles O. (for Oscar) Johnson's contribution to Minneapolis was major—major league sports, to be precise. Charlie Johnson retired in 1968 as executive sports editor of the Minneapolis *Star* after fifty years of covering sports news. It was through his needling and nudging that baseball's Minnesota Twins and football's Minnesota Vikings came to the area and settled down. Now in his seventies, he continues to promote sporting events as a consultant with the Chamber of Commerce.

Charlie Johnson is Swedish. So is Iner Johnson, a Swedish-born wholesale food salesman, who has been general chairman of *Svenskarnas Dag* festival for sixteen years. Iner has drawn the big crowds to the day-long event by booking in everybody Swedish from Hollywood's glamour-Swede, actress Ann-Margret, to Astronaut Edwin (Buzz) Aldrin. He was billed as "the first Swede on the moon."

The first woman ever elected to the Minneapolis city council was former alderman, Mrs. Elsa Johnson. Being married to a Johnson helped, of course, but her election opened the doors. Two other women have since been elected to the city council. One, Mrs. Gladys Brooks, continues to serve as alderman.

Perhaps the jolliest Johnson in Minneapolis was the late Charles (Charlie) Johnson, a great black entertainer of the 1890's. He made his name famous by inventing a dance called "the cakewalk." Johnson and his wife, the beautiful Dora Dean,

A very old photo of lumbering activities on Hennepin island, down-river from Nicollet island, in the Mississippi River (and under what is now the 3rd Ave. bridge. This picture shows a furniture factory, an old wooden bridge, Winslow House, the famed riverfront hotel, in the background. It was taken before 1870.

The Pence Opera House stood on Hennepin Ave., at 2nd St., on Bridge Square, until about 1960. It "died" with urban renewal even though it was in good condition and had, for many years, been well operated as the Union City Mission, a lodging house for elderly transients. On the site now is a well-landscaped park-like parking lot owned by Northwestern National Life Insurance Co., across Hennepin from it. Note the sign "Rothschilds." The store was the beginning for the Maurice L. Rothschild clothing store chain, now headquartered in Chicago. R. Rees was also clothing. I don't know about J. C. Oswald.

View of downtown Minneapolis in 1898 taken from courthouse tower
The building in foreground doesn't exist today, but was old New York
Life Insurance building at 5th St., and 2nd Ave. S.

Hennepin Ave., between 1st and 2nd Sts., in 1875. Left to right (back to front) are the Pence Opera house, T. K. Gray, pioneer druggist in mid-block, and the R. J. Mendenhall bank in right foreground. All buildings are now gone.

The first class of the Minneapolis School of Art—now the four-year accredited Minneapolis College of Art and Design. The college is currently building anew from designs by Kenzo Tange, renowned Japanese architect. This picture was taken when the art classes met on the top floor of the old Minneapolis public library at 10th St. and Hennepin Ave., now a parking lot. A very young J. Paul Getty remembers going up to the attic of the library and visiting the "school". The school was a part of the Minneapolis Society of Fine Arts which dates from 1880. It still is. The Society remains the governing body for the College and the city's major museum, the Minneapolis Institute of Arts.

toured the world and danced at the coronation of King Edward VII in 1901.

* * *

A few years ago, a newspaper public opinion poll asked readers to identify names of the most recognizable Minnesotans. Leading the list then was the late columnist for the Minneapolis *Star*, Cedric Adams. For twenty-five years, through his columns, radio and TV news broadcasts and public appearances, Adams was the best-known Minnesotan in and out of Minneapolis.

Senator Humphrey, of course, always has been easily identified in Minnesota. During an interview with the Senator at Macalester College, St. Paul, he shared with me some of his memories, hopes, and aspirations.

Hubert Horatio Humphrey was sixty-two on May 27, 1973, but the years don't show. He is as jaunty now as when he was the youngest mayor of Minneapolis in 1945.

It is only when he talks, and Humphrey has admitted that he enjoys talking, that you know he's been around. Humphrey is an experienced public servant. He has been Vice President of the United States and a nominee for President. Before that, he served Minnesota in the United States Senate.

In 1970, Minnesotans elected him to his fourth term in the Senate. Now, Humphrey is the "junior" senator from Minnesota. He revels in it and likes to point it out to crowds when he shares a platform with Minnesota's senior Senator Walter (Fritz) Mondale, who is 45. As a student, Mondale, also a Democrat, worked on Humphrey political campaigns.

When the 32-year-old Humphrey first made the run for mayor in 1943, he lost by 5,000 votes. Two years later, he tried again and won.

It was summer when I interviewed him. He was wearing a seersucker coat with slacks and a sporty necktie. He was ready to talk.

Question: Does it help to have Scandinavian ancestors to win an election for mayor of Minneapolis?

Humphrey: Oh, I think it does. (Smiles) I'm not sure it's a controlling factor, but it's a pleasant development. I used to have a difficult time convincing people in Minneapolis that I was part Scandinavian. After all, the name Humphrey doesn't lend itself to that interpretation.

My father used to joke about my public comments about my mother. He used to say, "How come you never mention me?"

"Well," I said, "Dad, you know Mom is the Norwegian in the family, and while I like the name of Humphrey, I don't know if it has any political plus in our community." (Laughs).

But truly, I think a name isn't that important today in modern politics, but it's on the positive side.

Question: Please recall your days as mayor. You were young, eager. You lost it once and then won. What did Minneapolis do for you and what did you do for the town?

Humphrey: I've always had a love affair with Minneapolis, even as a little boy. My first visit to the city was when I was in the eighth grade. I came with my father. Dad did business with the Minneapolis Drug Co. [His father was a pharmacist in Wallace, South Dakota, where Humphrey was born, and in Doland, South Dakota, where Humphrey graduated from high school in 1929 as class valedictorian.]

I recall our staying at the Andrews Hotel downtown. I remember seeing the big fire trucks go down the street. Minneapolis was my big city from the earliest days of my childhood. I came here as a University of Minnesota student in 1929, stayed a year, went back to South Dakota, and then came back again in 1937. Lived here ever since. I loved the university. I honestly have felt an indebtedness to the university that goes far beyond rational approach, I'm sure, because to me it was my opportunity. It just opened up every gate for me.

I ran for mayor in 1943 without too much feeling that I could win, but I wanted to do it. In the meantime, I'd done a great deal around the Twin Cities, teaching in adult education, working in local politics. When I was finally elected mayor, I thought I knew a great deal about our city, and I think I did. I was young and perceptive, active. Mrs. Humphrey and I loved it here. Our daughter, Nancy, was born in Swedish Hospital in 1939. Our son Skipper, (Hubert, the 3rd) was born in that same hospital. In fact, even our other two boys were born right here in Minneapolis.

So when I became mayor of Minneapolis, I was so pleased and excited about it and proud of the chance. I look back, recalling the articles I wrote, the speeches I made, the block work. I was a member of the Junior Chamber of Commerce and I worked in the labor movement with a workers' education program. You know, I think I spoke before every civic club in town even before I became mayor.

Question: But wasn't Minneapolis supposed to have been a wide-open and wild town when Humphrey came in and cleaned it up? Isn't that the old story?

Humphrey: That was the old story, but compared to other great cities, it wasn't THAT wide open. But there was a good deal of illicit, illegal activity, mostly small-time cheating and some gambling . . . booking. We appointed Ed Ryan as chief of police. [Ryan, a six-foot, five-inch Irishman who speaks fluent French, thanks to the French bride he brought home from World War I, later served many years as Hennepin County Sheriff.] Ryan was a strict law enforcement man and a wonderful public relations man as well. A tremendous personality. The two of us worked together like a real team.

Oh, I had dreams for this city. I remember, we designed the first lower loop redevelopment program. We had architectural drawings made, and I was a member of the city planning commission and took a great interest in that. I also served on the park board and as chairman of the public welfare committee. We did things during those years.

Question: You weren't frustrated by our nineteenth-century city charter?

Humphrey: True, the charter doesn't give the mayor a great deal of authority, but as mayor, you're the number one citizen. If you use the mayor's office to promote the good of the community, I think you can get a lot of things done.

We set up all sorts of citizens' commissions and committees.

I was able to get the late Rev. Reuben Youngdahl as chairman of our human relations commission even though his brother, Luther, was the Republican governor of Minnesota then. [Until his death, Rev. Youngdahl was pastor of Minneapolis' Mount Olivet Lutheran Church. With a membership of 10,000, it is the largest Lutheran Church in the United States.]

We passed the first fair employment practices ordinance with enforcement powers. We set up the citizens' financial and tax committee that looked into our entire city tax structure. We also had a law enforcement committee, a veterans' affairs committee, a traffic committee—all private citizens, but bringing in some government people. This is how I tried to work out the concept of partnership between government and the private sector right from the beginning.

Question: You had bipartisan support as mayor—true?

Humphrey: You bet I did. As a matter of fact, when I ran for re-election in 1947, I had the president of the Chamber of Commerce, the president of the A. F. of L., the president of the Junior Chamber of Commerce and the president of the C.I.O. as my campaign co-chairmen.

I loved being mayor of Minneapolis. I really did. I think I loved that job more than anything in my life. I could see things happen. I could see how to make a better city out of it and get a better spirit going with the people. After all, every city is like a person. It has a personality.

Question: What is Minneapolis' personality?

Humphrey: I think our personality is an upbeat one. It's not a rambunctious personality, but it's a kind of a healthy, positive glow. Steady optimism, I'd say. And there is really not a great deal of disenchantment and bitterness here, although there has been more of it in recent years because of racial difficulties.

Question: In 1946, while you were mayor, wasn't Minneapolis singled out as the most anti-Semitic city in the United States?

Humphrey: Yes. Carey McWilliams, a famous commentator on sociological problems, did say that Minneapolis was one of the two most anti-Semitic cities. We conducted a community self-survey with outside experts. It lasted a year. Teams of our own citizens worked with them to examine the social attitudes and practices of the medical profession, the labor movement, the business community, social institutions, churches—everything. We published an amazing report and held public meetings with it. For example, we found that in some of the hospitals even then, if you were not a Protestant or if you were not Caucasian, you couldn't practice medicine in those hospitals. We put a big mirror over Minneapolis in a sense and we looked up into it and occasionally saw our own dirty faces. And we began to clean it up right then.

[At that time, there were few blacks in the business offices or retail stores and members of the Jewish faith were rarely found in banking or brokerage offices.

That has been completely turned around, but the cause, led by many involved civic leaders of all races, continues.

The city's oldest club, the Minneapolis Club, took in its first Jewish members in 1962 and admitted its first black members in 1968. Service clubs such as Rotary and Kiwanis have also admitted minority members in recent years. Most of the city's country clubs continue to be exclusive, however. Today it is the American Indian who remains in many cases the major underprivileged minority in Minneapolis. Now, with some financial help from the community, the Indians are independently working to help their own people.]

I think maybe the best thing we did during my mayorship was this community human relations survey. I think it did something to cleanse us in terms of our social, economic and political practices.

Question: What is our biggest problem today? If you were mayor of Minneapolis now, what would you want to do?

Humphrey: I would say that our Twin Cities of Minneapolis and St. Paul are rather healthy, wholesome communities compared to other large cities. Every problem we have is manageable. It is not beyond our control if we have the will and we apply the resources. Now I realize that the finance problem is a critical problem for cities. And there are two or three ways to get at it.

One way, of course, is to get tax sharing—not just federal to state, but state to local. A certain percentage of the sales tax could be dedicated to municipalities.

But one of the best ways is to increase the tax base and improve the tax base of the city. That doesn't mean raising tax rates. To the contrary, our property tax rates are exorbitantly high. We're going to be able to alter those rates primarily by federal assistance and state assistance, particularly in education.

Question: Does this mean that we need more new business buildings such as the IDS Tower in Minneapolis?

Humphrey: Yes, it does, but even more important we need to have industry built where there are people for the jobs. Instead of industry fleeing to the suburbs, I think it is important that we have rezoning in our cities and tax incentives and that we use the power of the Mayor's office and the power of the city council to literally entice and encourage industry to build their plants where the work force is—in the inner city. And you must have decent neighborhoods around them. You can have a modern industrial plant in a residential area today without any pollution or contamination. It's all a matter of planning—for landscaping, parking, recreation facilities. This is done in Europe. It can be done here, and I think it is needed.

Question: When you're in Washington, what do you miss most about Minneapolis?

Humphrey: I miss above all the kind of gentle nature of our city—the parks, even in winter, and particularly in summer. The Lake of the Isles area. Lake Calhoun and Lake Nokomis. All of these different, wonderful beautiful lakes that we have right in town and all of our parkways. We have lots of park space in the Twin Cities and particularly in Minneapolis. We're indebted to old Theodore Wirth for that. [Wirth was superintendent of the parks in Minneapolis for about thirty years.]

In our parks we have public golf clubs. When you compare that to other cities, it's hard to believe. We have provided living space and recreation space, and I tell you when you get away from here, you sense the difference right away. Sure, we have big buildings. We have steel and concrete, but we don't have jungles of it. We break it up with open spaces, trees, shrubbery, lawns, parks and plazas.

Question: Do you think we'll save Minneapolis from becoming a concrete jungle?

Humphrey: Yes, I think we can save it here. With other big cities, we really just have to rebuild them. When we plan now for new housing developments in Minneapolis, I want to make sure we plan them with plenty of living space. Private industry alone can't afford this. There must be public help, and that's why urban renewal programs must reach out beyond the business districts. We must provide private developers with large amounts of land at prices they can afford so that they can sell to private owners. We ought to make public housing beautiful. I'm so fed up with the semi-prison-style architecture. Public housing, all public buildings ought to be the best. I tell you that if you make public housing beautiful, you can make people in public housing beautiful. They react accordingly. And we don't need it all high-rise. It's not as if we didn't have plenty of land here. And we should provide social services, see that garbage is picked up, lawns are cared for, then people get accustomed to picking up debris and keeping neighborhoods looking pretty.

Question: How about opening up the riverfront downtown?

Humphrey: Oh, isn't it a pity that we've let that beautiful Mississippi river become industrial! Why, the recreation that is possible along there. We need marinas and piers for fishing and for restaurants. The Mississippi river is a God-sent gift to us. We ought to make the most of it. [An urban task force of city planners is currently working on plans toward that end.]

Question: Finally, what do you see for Minneapolis and the metropolitan area in 1990?

Humphrey: I think we're now going through a rather important series of governmental adjustments. I think there are a number of responsibilities that will have to be taken over by the Metropolitan Council. Today cities need sufficient authority in legal jurisdiction to be responsive to the people. And while I doubt that suburban communities are going to want to give up their

Another look at the milling (lumber milling) district as it was between 1860-70.

The old (and original) Nicollet House hotel at Nicollet Ave., and Washington Ave. The current Pick-Nicollet Hotel occupies the same site. It dates from 1924.

The Rothschilds also operated the Palace. I don't know if they did in 1888 when this picture was taken.

The Winslow House was the fabled hotel on the east bank of the Mississippi River in what was the village of St. Anthony. Before the Civil War, it was a deluxe hotel, catering to Southern families who came up river with slaves to escape summer heat. It was built in 1856-57, was six stories high and then, largest west of Chicago. After and during the Civil War, business failed. It housed Macalester College (now in St. Paul) in the 1870s and was used in the 1880s as a hospital. It was razed in 1886 for the Exposition building which housed the GOP national convention in 1892. That building went down during WW II. The local Coca Cola plant now occupies the magnificent river site, more's the pity.

identities, I think we ought to be sufficiently innovative to provide certain community services that are uniform and are done collectively, such as sewage disposal and public transit. We've learned how to put together group health programs, and we still have our doctors.

There is a great opportunity in metropolitan government for advanced planning—to repair obsolescence within the city and out in the suburbs. And I see a need for it, by the way. You take Highway 12 going west out of town. [The highway leads to Lake Minnetonka and the plush lakeside villages where many Minneapolis business and civic leaders live. It also leads to Humphrey's Waverly, Minnesota, lakeside home forty miles from downtown.] It's a hodgepodge that ought not to be. Now, the state government has got to plan or give the county authority and the mandate to plan or you've got to permit the Metropolitan Council to do that planning and zoning. You can't afford to let a great vast area just out of town become a combination of hot dog stands, filling stations, apartment houses, offices, industrial plants—without any rhyme or reason. This has happened. It will have to be changed, and that is costly. The time to zone is early. And we ought to have belts of open space dividing our city and its suburbs. When you divide them by nature, you provide places for people to escape in a sense. Old London is surrounded by a green belt. It's like a virgin wilderness. There are even deer there and flowers, trees, shrubbery—and not a hot dog stand anyplace. We've got to do that.

Just then, one of Humphrey's aides came in to signal the end of the interview. Humphrey, who had made two speeches just before it, set off to a TV station for another go-around. En route, he would be interviewed in the car by a reporter from the Los Angeles *Times*. That night, he would make a couple of more public appearances.

Walking briskly to the car, he talked about how proud he was that Mrs. Humphrey—the former Muriel Buck, whom Humphrey married in 1936—was to receive the humanitarian award that week from *Svenskarnas Dag* for her work with the mentally retarded.

At the car, he waved good-bye, climbed in and started right in talking to the *Times* reporter. He looked very, very happy as he rode away.

* * *

Take to the lakes when you arrive in Minneapolis. Canoe them. Snowshoe them, if the weather is right. Hike, ride a bike, take a bus or drive, but whatever you do, see the lake districts first.

After a look, make for the Mississippi River downtown, where Minneapolis began. Put on your walking shoes because the Nicollet Mall is nearby.

To begin at the beginning, the best spot from which to start a tour of Minneapolis is at the lookout platform atop the lock and dam on the riverbank. Inside the observation platform is a bronze plaque that will help you find the points of interest to be seen from up there.

Across the river in front of you is the Pillsbury "A" mill. When the creamy limestone building opened in 1881, it was the largest flour mill in the world. Today, although used by the Pillsbury Co. only for storage and shipping, it is one of Minneapolis's major landmarks. Dr. Donald Torbert, architectural historian at the University of Minnesota, said of it: "If any one building now extant may be said to be at the center of the city's history, it is the Pillsbury 'A'." Harrison Salisbury, a New York *Times* editor, agrees. Salisbury, a former Minneapolitan, worked in the mill as a young man. "One way or another," Salisbury said, "it should be saved, because frankly there is nothing so characteristic of Minneapolis, so symbolic of what made the city, than the old Pillsbury 'A'."

The "A" mill overlooks another of Minneapolis' most cherished landmarks—the stone arch bridge. It was contributed to the river and Minneapolis by the St. Paul railroad magnate, Jim Hill. Constructed of the same creamy limestone as the mill, the bridge opened to railroad traffic in 1884. It is still in daily use.

On the far side of the stone arch bridge, about a block down Main Street from the mill, is Lucy Wilder Morris Park. From there, history claims, Father Louis Hennepin first saw St. Anthony Falls in 1680. The mill and the park are on the St. Anthony Village side of the river. Remember, St. Anthony was on the right or east bank of the Mississippi going upstream.

Another landmark on the east bank is Our Lady of Lourdes Catholic Church. The church, oldest in Minneapolis, was built by the Universalists in 1855. Although its facade and its interior have been altered, its foundation stands firm.

The oldest house in Minneapolis is also on the St. Anthony side of the river. The Ard Godfrey cottage, built in 1848, is in Richard Chute Square, not far from the church. Unfortunately, it is presently boarded up and not open to tours as it once was. If plans for the future work out, the Godfrey cottage could be moved to nearby Nicollet Island and become a part of a historic village.

Since the beginning of the twentieth century, the island, covering forty-eight acres in the middle of the Mississippi in the center of downtown Minneapolis, has been the city's most neglected treasure. Before the turn of the century, it was one of the city's aristocratic residential districts. Then industry moved in, followed by missions and soup kitchens. Today, Minneapolis city planners are working on ideas to return Nicollet Island to the mainstream of city activity. Plans include a historic village for tourists. Nearby will be new housing for Minneapolis residents.

Private development has already refurbished one building on the east bank down the block from the "A" mill on Main St. Southeast. It houses an attractive bar and restaurant complete with open air dining facilities for summer and a skylighted indoor "garden" for summer or winter.

When you leave the observation tower and the riverbank, you walk under one of the land-based arches of the stone arch bridge. It makes a dandy background for photographs, and if the weeds aren't too high, so does the old millstone that stands at the top of the street leading away from the lock and dam. It's another neglected relic of Minneapolis' past.

En route to the Nicollet Mall, visit the 1900-vintage Minneapolis Grain Exchange, the largest cash grain market in the world.

Across the street from the Exchange is the magnificent Minneapolis city hall-courthouse. Since it went up in 1889, the building, with its tall clock tower, has dominated the city skyline. For fifty-seven years, until his death in 1969, Joseph Henry Auld, a Minneapolis piano tuner, played the tower chimes on holidays and special occasions. Until an elevator was installed in 1947, Auld walked the 242 steps up to the tower. One special occasion when the chimes rang out was during the Minneapolis premiere of Mike Todd's *Around the World in 80 Days*. To serenade the hometown boy who made good, Auld played the movie's famous theme song on the chimes. Since Auld's death, his son, Edward, has taken over the job.

The chimes have been automated, thanks to funds raised by a group of businessmen headed by George Dayton, and Auld's electrified keyboard is now on the building's ground floor.

The interior of the city hall-courthouse is a fascinating maze of hallways, offices, elegant courtrooms and the jail. The lobby on the 4th Street side of the building—complete with its stained glass windows and marble statue of the Father of Waters—is almost unchanged in 85 years.

John Carl Warnecke, the San Francisco architect who designed the new Hennepin County Government Center across the street, hopes the two structures will enhance each other. At no time was consideration given to razing the old building. To most residents, it is an untouchable landmark.

Now for the Nicollet Mall, Minneapolis' marketplace, and its answer to the suburban shopping center. Nicollet Avenue was Minneapolis' main shopping street for sixty years. When suburban centers began to draw crowds, downtown merchants and civic leaders decided to do something about it.

Laurence Halprin, San Francisco landscape architect, was hired to redesign the avenue. He created the Mall specifically for pedestrians and transit buses. The twenty-four-foot-wide roadway edged by spacious sidewalks (heated in winter to melt snow and ice instantly) winds and curves for eight blocks.

Mrs. Hubert H. Humphrey helped scoop up the first shovel of dirt to start the refurbishing in 1966. Mrs. Lyndon B. Johnson dedicated the Mall during one of her beautification tours in 1968. Since then, the Mall has received national acclaim from urban designers as one of the handsomest shopping streets in the United States.

Start walking at Washington Avenue and the Mall, at the north end or the "top" of the promenade. Note as you walk that the Mall is dotted in every block with fountains, benches, flower beds, trees, heated bus shelters, sculpture and, regularly, special events such as art shows, concerts and folk festivals.

Washington Avenue and the Mall is a corner loved by amateur photographers. One reason is the graceful pavilion designed by Minoru Yamasaki for the headquarters of the Northwestern National Life Insurance Co. The pavilion is surrounded by pools and a garden of sculpture in black Japanese granite by sculptor Masayuki Nagare. On the building's elegant portico, a visitor can look into the lobby, where a fourteen by forty-six-foot lacy metal sculpture by Harry Bertoia dominates the area.

A plaza connects the insurance building with the new 500-unit luxury apartment complex, the Towers. It is surrounded by gardens containing tennis courts and a swimming pool. Along the Hennepin Avenue side of the apartments is a fountain of "dancing waters," complete with multicolored lights.

The setting draws tourists both summer and winter, and has even been used as the background for an outdoor wedding. Concerts and theatrical performances are also staged on the plaza near the fountain.

Directly across Washington Avenue at the Mall corner is another spectacular new building. The Federal Reserve Bank is the first suspension building in the world. The design by architect Gunnar Birkerts borrows an idea from suspension bridge construction. The bank hangs on cables thirty feet above a plaza—suspended between two towers. A third tower for

Hennepin Ave. side of old Nicollet House. You can note in earlier photo that windows are curved on the Nicollet Ave. corner and straight in this one. I don't know which section was the oldest.

Shot looking north on Washington Ave., at corner of Marquette Ave. Nicollet is the next street north. The drug store is Murison & Co. J. S. Elliot dealt in "music and jewelry." Between 1860-70, Washington Ave., was the main street of the city.

Downstream from the milling district, but still in city, is this scene showing the old Bohemian Flats section of town. Bridge going up is probably an old railroad bridge now gone. In the background can be seen James J. Hill's famous stone arch bridge (1883) which is still standing and used. Probably taken in the mid-80s.

(*Minnesota Historical Society*)

St. Mark's Episcopal church, when it stood on 6th St., between Nicollet and Hennepin, where Dyckman Hotel now stands. Picture taken in the late 1860s.

elevators isn't involved in holding the building up. The load the twelve-story building will put on the towers is 56,520,000 pounds. People who calculate such things say that the bank will weigh as much as 158 empty Boeing 747 airplanes.

Since the bank didn't move into the building until the late summer of 1973, the effect a stiff and typical Minneapolis wind will have on the people inside the swinging structure is yet to be known.

The plaza around the building will climb twenty-two feet from its low point on the Mall side to Marquette Avenue, a block away. Under the plaza will be the bank vaults and a garage.

On the plaza are benches, a grove of Linden trees, three pieces of monumental sculpture by three young American artists—Paul Granlund, Dimitri Hadzi and Charles Perry—and a 125-foot-long "river" fountain by Birkerts.

Before leaving the corner of Washington and the Mall, look at the Pick-Nicollet Hotel across from the bank. There has been a Nicollet House on that corner since the 1850's. The present hotel, the second Nicollet, dates from 1924.

The Mall between 3rd and 4th Streets: bordered on one side by the new Minneapolis public library. At the library entrance is a small plaza with a pool and a sculpture by John Rood, a

(Left) The famous first "skyscraper" west of Chicago—the NW Guarantee Loan Co., built in 1889 by Louis Menage. Later and most famously known as the Metropolitan Life Insurance building. Attempts were made to preserve it when it fell into hands of urban renewal in the late 1950s. It was razed for a parking lot. I might add that its floors were glass around much-wrought-iron-ed central court. A great architectural loss. It stood on 3rd St., at 2nd Ave. S. Looking to the right down 3rd St., toward Marquette Ave., is the old Federal Courts building. It was razed in urban renewal for new federal courts building on same site. Looking left up 2nd Ave. S., you see the tall building background which is the old New York Life Insurance Co. building at 5th St., where the First National Bank of Minneapolis now stands. Menage, by the way, "lost" his company and almost his neck. He had to light out to South America.

(Library of Congress)

former member of the faculty at the University of Minnesota. Inside the library, visit the science museum and planetarium. And don't miss the Minneapolis Athenaeum's library of rare antique books, also inside the main building. The Minneapolis Athenaeum Society was Minneapolis' first library. It is still maintained by private funds.

Across from the library is the elegant Sheraton-Ritz Hotel. Architect Robert Cerny of Minneapolis designed the Hotel complex complete with a parking ramp, outdoor pool and garden cafe. A bank and several shops are also a part of the hotel.

The Mall between 4th and 5th Streets: On one side is the Florentine palazzo of Northern States Power Co. (NSP), designed by architect Pietro Belluschi of the Massachusetts Institute of Technology. A large plaza with a pool and plantings opens onto the Mall from the building. The Minnesota Orchestra has played concerts on the plaza, and other special events are also staged there.

The best shopping in the Upper Midwest begins on the Mall at Powers, just across the Mall from NSP. The store's sidewalk cafe under the trees is an attractive spot for lunch. Across 5th Street from NSP is more good shopping, as well as the Minneapolis Chamber of Commerce building with its convention and visitors' bureau.

The Mall between 5th and 6th Streets: Penney's dominates the block on one side of the avenue. A block of small shops lines the Mall across from it.

The Mall between 6th and 7th Streets: Donaldson's department store covers the block from 6th to 7th. The section on the 6th Street corner dates back to the 19th century when Donaldson's Glass Block was the city's most elegant store. Across from it are more specialty shops and the home service center of the Minneapolis Gas Co., known as Minnegasco.

On Minnegasco's front stoop, gas-heated in winter, is an old-fashioned popcorn wagon owned and operated by a cheerful widow, Mrs. Charlotte Sunderlin. In winter, with help from a Minnegasco gas grill, Mrs. Sunderlin also sells hot roasted chestnuts.

The Mall between 7th and 8th Streets: Dayton's department store covers the west side of the block.

Across the Mall from Dayton's and connected to it by skyway is the new IDS Center. Skyways also radiate from the IDS crystal court to connect with Donaldson's, the International Multifoods building and Midwest Federal Savings & Loan Co.

Dayton's is also connected by skyway to the LaSalle Court, a shopping arcade and parking ramp across 8th Street from the store. Another arcade connects the store to the Radisson Hotel on 7th Street. A skyway and an underground tunnel across 7th Street connects the hotel to the Radisson Merchandise Mart.

Five more skyways and two tunnels for a total of 11 skyways and three tunnels are now in use downtown with a 12th skyway scheduled to be built in 1974.

To date, the system connects 12 square blocks. By 1985, skyways will connect 54 downtown blocks.

The Mall between 8th and 9th Streets: The Midwest Federal building at 8th and the Mall was designed by the Minneapolis architectural firm of Peterson, Clark & Griffith. Midwest Federal's president, Harold W. Greenwood Jr., is former president of the Minnesota United Nations Association. That's why the flags of the United Nations often fly from special flagpoles attached to the building. The building's plaza is the site of the Eddie Webster's Pub, a sidewalk cafe.

Across from the plaza is another row of good stores including Harold's, for women's clothes. Up a block and across from Harold's is Albrecht's, a family business that began when fur traders were first bringing their pelts into St. Paul from northern Minnesota. The Minneapolis branch of the firm sells women's clothes as well as fine furs.

One shouldn't leave the corner of 8th and the Mall without taking a few steps down 8th Street to visit Maud Borup's. Royal families of Europe are among its candy customers. So are most Minneapolis families, who, until six years ago, had to buy their Maud Borup candies at the original store in St. Paul. When Maud Borup's moved across the river, Minneapolitans were grateful.

The Mall between 9th and 10th Streets: Young-Quinlan's, often described as one of the most beautiful store buildings in the world, stands at 9th and the Mall. The Young-Quinlan store, opened in 1926, was the culmination of a dream for Elizabeth C. Quinlan, a young Irish girl who started clerking as a teen-ager in a Nicollet Avenue store. In 1894, with a fellow clerk named Fred C. Young, she opened Young-Quinlan, the first ready-to-wear women's shop in Minneapolis. Although Young died early in their partnership, she always retained his name. Before her death in 1947, Miss Quinlan won national fame—including a citation from *Time Magazine*—for her innovations in retailing.

The store's architecture was influenced by Miss Quinlan's love for Florence, Italy. She also believed that a store should provide beautiful surroundings for shoppers. The Italianate palazzo on 9th Street is the result. And her own residence in Minneapolis' lovely Kenwood district was of a similar design.

Her idea of offering merchandise in special little shops or "boutiques" within one big store has been continued by subsequent owners. The building itself is one of Minneapolis' most attractive landmarks.

Attached to the Young-Quinlan building is another landmark on Nicollet. It is a remarkable fabric store named Amluxen's. It was opened in 1927 by George E. Amluxen, now 95. Amluxen began his retailing career at Donaldson's in 1897. Today, Amluxen's grandson runs the store, although its founder still comes in almost daily to greet customers. Amluxen no longer travels around the world to buy fine fabrics for Minneapolis seamstresses, but he makes certain that his grandson still provides the best in yardgoods.

Specialty shops line the Mall to the 10th Street corner. Presently, city planners are working on designs to extend the Mall about six more blocks to Loring Park.

On the 11th Street corner, construction is underway on the new orchestra hall.

The landmark at the 10th Street corner of the Mall is Roy H. Bjorkman, a fashion pace-setter on Nicollet for 50 years. Bjorkman, now 80, is semi-retired from the women's apparel store that bears his name. His sons, Roy and Edwin, carry on the family retailing tradition.

Occasionally, for an old customer, Bjorkman, Sr., will work his special brand of salesmanship. Until you've watched him sell a fur coat—flinging an expensive mink or sable on the carpeted floor with a theatrical flair—you don't know what old-fashioned showmanship in merchandising really is.

Before striking out from downtown, there are several other sites and sights worth seeing.

One of the prettiest blocks downtown is on 2nd Avenue South, between 7th and 8th Streets. On the corner is the green glass building of the Lutheran Brotherhood Insurance Co. If you stop in, you will have a chance to see its lovely back garden. Next to it is the ivy-entwined Minneapolis Club, the city's oldest men's club. Big business meets and eats there every day of every week.

Across from the club is the modern St. Olaf Catholic Church. The chimes in its bell tower toll several times daily, as do the bells of First Baptist Church and Gethsemane Episcopal Church, both historic 19th-century buildings downtown. The Northwestern National Bank and Midwest Federal also provide regular carillon concerts. The city hall chimes play on national holidays.

When all of the bells and chimes begin clanging together—and they do on some noon hours—the result is clamorous, but never uncomfortably so.

Looming above downtown since 1929 has been the Foshay Tower, a silly-looking but beloved landmark. It's a business building that is patterned after the Washington Monument. Until 1973, the thirty-two story Foshay was the tallest building in the five-state Upper Midwest area, including western Wisconsin, the Dakotas and Montana. Now, the "tallest" designation belongs to the 57-story IDS Center.

Minneapolis' main entertainment street is Hennepin Avenue. It has looked somewhat frowzy for years, but city planners and downtown businessmen regularly talk about refurbishing it.

There are several other churches downtown worth a look. Among them are Gethsemane Episcopal, Wesley Methodist,

Central Lutheran, Westminster Presbyterian, and First Baptist.

Downtown Minneapolis also boasts seven public swimming pools. They are open to hotel residents and their guests. Outdoor pools are available at the Sheraton-Ritz, and the Curtis. Indoor pools are open at the Curtis, the Northstar, the Holiday Inn, the Hyatt House and the Normandy.

Members can swim at the YMCA, YWCA, Minneapolis Club and Minneapolis Athletic Club. If you just want to dunk your feet, there are six fountains on the Nicollet Mall. You'll have a better chance of getting away with it if you're a pretty girl, however.

At the edge of downtown is Loring Park, a pretty green space edged by apartment buildings, Metropolitan State Junior College and two more historic churches.

The Catholic Basilica of St. Mary and the Episcopal Cathedral Church of St. Mark are both on the list of important Minneapolis landmarks, as is Hennepin Avenue United Methodist church, just up Lowry Hill from St. Mark's. Across from St. Mark's are the new Walker Art Center and the Tyrone Guthrie Theatre.

Most of downtown Minneapolis can be seen on foot. The following sites will take wheels.

THE BETTY CROCKER KITCHENS OF GENERAL MILLS: Yes, Betty is alive and well and cooking with cake mixes.

DUNWOODY INDUSTRIAL INSTITUTE: A fine technical school complete with a marvelous bakery selling fresh delectables daily.

VOCATIONAL HIGH SCHOOL AND TECHNICAL INSTITUTE: A public school that features a store stocked with student-made merchandise.

ELOISE BUTLER WILDFLOWER GARDEN: Wild plants native to three Minnesota areas bloom here. The garden is also a bird refuge and a Minneapolis treasure.

LAKE HARRIET ROSE GARDENS: A summertime showplace.

MINNEHAHA PARK: Drive there via Minnehaha Parkway along Minnehaha Creek (or rubber-raft it in the spring). The creek ends at Minnehaha Falls in the park. Also there is the John Stevens

Corner of 6th St. and Nicollet about 1890. 5th St. is down Nicollet
to your left. The old 1882-built Grand Opera House is at the right on
6th St., with sign out front advertising Boston Lyric Opera. In foreground facing both 6th and Nicollet was Heffelfinger's shoe store. It
is one of city's oldest names. The Heffelfinger family is still very
involved in city today. The store was on the street floor of the Syndicate
Block. Upper floors were occupied then by the YMCA.

house, first dwelling on the west bank of the Mississippi in Minneapolis. At the edge is the restored Minnehaha railroad depot.

FORT SNELLING: The fort, completed in 1827, has been splendidly restored by the Minnesota Historical Society. It is one of the major sights to see not only in Minneapolis, but in the United States.

BRIDAL VEIL FALLS: This is one sight many residents forget to show visitors. It is at the east end of the Franklin Avenue bridge across the Mississippi. There's a good view of it from the west bank.

AMERICAN SWEDISH INSTITUTE: Swan Turnblad's castle. Definitely worth a stop.

MINNEAPOLIS INSTITUTE OF ARTS: The major public museum.

HENNEPIN COUNTY HISTORICAL SOCIETY: It looks like Charley Hoag's attic. Everything you want to know about old Minneapolis is here, just across from the Art Institute.

MINNEAPOLIS COLLEGE OF ART AND DESIGN: The fine four-year arts college is adjacent to the Institute. In May everybody attends the student-sponsored "Clothesline" art show.

CHARLES S. PILLSBURY MANSION: Built in 1912 by the milling magnate, the house contains rooms and woodwork from Elizabethan and Jacobean English manor houses. It is now owned by the Minneapolis Society of Fine Arts.

WALKER ART CENTER: It contains one of the best collections of contemporary art in the United States.

TYRONE GUTHRIE THEATRE: Seeing is believing in repertory theater.

CHRIST LUTHERAN CHURCH: A contemporary architectural landmark dating from 1950. It was designed by architects Eliel and Eero Saarinen.

PLYMOUTH CONGREGATIONAL CHURCH: Another turn-of-the-century architectural landmark.

Nicollet at 5th St., looking up toward 6th and that's the Syndicate Block, again, in the left background. About 1900.

UNIVERSITY OF MINNESOTA: An educational mammoth. Among the sights to see are the James Ford Bell Museum of Natural History, the James Ford Bell library of rare books, Pillsbury Hall (for its period architectural excellence), the University Showboat (in summer), the collection of twentieth century American art (atop Northrop Auditorium), Coffman Union, the Variety Club Heart Hospital, Mayo Memorial building, Masonic Memorial Hospital, and the new Performing Arts Center. (On the St. Paul campus, there are all sorts of domestic animals being tended by agricultural students.)

AUGSBURG COLLEGE: A century-old four-year liberal arts college founded by Norwegian Lutherans in one of Minneapolis's oldest sections of town, Cedar-Riverside. Cedar-Riverside is now the setting for a redevelopment project combining old and new buildings and known as the "new town, in town."

MINNEAPOLIS BREWING CO: Beer is still brewed in the dandy old nineteenth-century building. Visitors can sample the beer in the adjacent Grainbelt (beer) park with its fountain and live deer.

METROPOLITAN SPORTS CENTER AND STADIUM: This is where the Twins, the Vikings and the North Stars play baseball, football and hockey. During the football season, the parking lot is the scene of what is claimed to be the biggest outdoor tailgate picnic in the world.

Nearby in the western suburbs you'll find:

LAKE MINNETONKA: Big and busy in summer and winter. At Excelsior on the lake is the Old Log Theater, a professional acting company that performs all year 'round.

THE ENSCULPTIC HOUSE: Designed by architect Eliot Winslow Wedin, son of the well-known Minneapolis artist, Elof Wedin, the house is a free-form masterpiece of modern materials, including Fiberglas and plastic foam. It is open to public tours on certain days.

JONATHAN: A "new town" being built from the ground up. Tourists are welcome.

MINNESOTA ABORETUM: Open space, green and good-smelling and carefully tended. There is a place to picnic, and there are naturalist guides on duty.

There are many historic structures, art galleries, craft shops, and just plain interesting places to see in and near Minneapolis.

Don't try to view everything at once. Take time—particularly in spring, summer and fall—to return to the shores of the city lakes and practice your loafing. Don't forget, though, to allow yourself plenty of time to go to the restaurants.

Most restaurants are family-owned, serving good food in every style from middle-western American to Japanese. Curiously for Minneapolis, no restaurant regularly features an authentic Scandinavian smorgasbord. To eat Norwegian *lefse* and Swedish fruit soup, you have to wedge your way in to the Sons of Norway lodge hall on Sunday afternoons. Their smorgasbord table is worth the crowd.

It is on the historical record that Minneapolitans have eaten well since 1862 when Fred Schiek opened a "genteel" dining room on Washington Av., the city's main street until the 20th century. Schiek, a German or a Swiss—nobody ever knew for sure—served sauerbraten and kartoffel pfankuchen (potato pancakes) to everybody. Sarah Bernhardt and Lillian Russell always ate there, though never together.

Schiek's moved only twice during its more than 100 years in business. Fred Schiek's son, Louis, operated the restaurant after his father died in 1906. After Louis died, the business was sold to Benjamin H. Berger, Minneapolis movie theater owner and sports entrepreneur.

Berger owned the restaurant from 1943 until 1972 when he decided to close its doors permanently. Fortunately, the historic bank building that was the last home of Schiek's can still be seen. It now houses an Italian restaurant.

Berger closed Schiek's because it had lost money for the first time in the almost 30 years he owned it. He also needed time for his movie business and his volunteer activities. Berger, who originally owned the Minneapolis Lakers professional basketball team, now in Los Angeles, is a member of the state parole board and a Minneapolis park commissioner. In 1972, he donated a $100,000 fountain to the city.

Minneapolis' other culinary landmark is still going strong after only 40 years. It is Charlie's Cafe Exceptionale, a restaurant with a national reputation that has landed it on Holiday magazine's list of "best restaurants" annually since the list began.

Minneapolitans refuse to do without Charlie's. Since Charlie Herlin and Charlie Saunders opened it in an old mansion on December 16, 1933, it has been a success.

Herlin died in 1934. For the next thirty years, Saunders—a soft-spoken, Minneapolis-born *bon vivant*—was Charlie's Charlie. He loved good food, good wine and good company, and worked hard at creating the proper setting for it.

When Saunders wasn't at his restaurant, he was flying. He was a ferry pilot for the air transport command during World War II. His other favorite hobby was raising harness race horses. Harness racing, a grand, old-fashioned midwestern sport, led Saunders to build a half-mile track on his 300-acre farm in suburban Bloomington.

In 1959 Saunders married Louise Herou, an attractive Minneapolis lawyer, championship golfer, and, in her teens, a trophy-winning speed skater. Mrs. Saunders was a member of a famous Minneapolis law firm. Another member, Orville Freeman, went on to the state capital as governor and then to Washington in the Johnson Cabinet. Minnesota Congressman Don Fraser and Lee Loevinger, former FCC commissioner, also were members of the firm. Louise Saunders didn't plan to run a restaurant. Public opinion, in and out of Minneapolis, changed her mind.

When her husband died in 1964, Mrs. Saunders decided to sell Charlie's. In 1966, with a buyer ready to sign, Mrs. Saunders announced her decision. The hue and cry was overwhelming, reaching into the Minneapolis city council chambers, where aldermen have the power to accept or reject liquor license transfers. Since the aldermen were hearing from Charlie's customers too, they were not eager to transfer the license to the new owner. The upshot of the hullabaloo was that Mrs. Saunders changed her mind and didn't sell. "Our restaurant is a family," she said recently. "Our employees had spent the better parts of their lives creating this restaurant with my husband.

James J. Hill (the Empire Builder of the Great Northern railroad) built this magnificent stone arch bridge to open in 1883. It still stands across the Mississippi River and is used. On the east bank of the river is the Pillsbury "A" mill, near right, and in the background, the building with the tower is the Exposition building, which replaced the Winslow House, and housed the 1892 GOP convention.

"The letters, the phone calls, the personal pleas from friends and strangers made selling all too complicated. I decided I'd better forget my law practice and learn the restaurant business."

That she has done with zest and a good calorie counter, traveling coast to coast and throughout the world eating, always eating, at the best restaurants. Mrs. Saunders also visits all of the great vineyards regularly, to sample personally the wines she buys. The wine cellar is excellent, and it includes, because Louise Saunders believes in them, a goodly assortment of American wines.

"My husband was a man's man and in the earlier days, Charlie's was a kind of men's club where the men enjoyed having the ladies join them as guests occasionally.

"This was a meat, potatoes and bourbon town thirty years ago. That's changed. Today some customers still like their meat, potatoes and bourbon, but just as many enjoy and prefer gourmet dishes."

Although Charlie's is always an elegant place to dine, there is an air of midwestern hospitality about it that keeps the homefolks happy. Every year from November through January, the menu offers *lefse* and *lutfisk* daily. Wild rice, a typical Minnesota-grown product that Easterners and Westerners adore, is available anytime.

In 1948 Charlie's moved out of the old mansion and into a new building that Saunders planned and designed. "He not only planned, he even helped install the kitchen appliances," Mrs. Saunders recalled, "He loved working with tools. Anytime anything went wrong in the kitchen, he would be there doing the repairs himself."

Mrs. Saunders believes that Minneapolis has the best restaurants in the midwest and that they can rival many in such cities as New York or San Francisco. Charlie's own cheesecake, for example, is as creamy as any in its natural habitat of Manhattan. Steak Diane is a usual entree. So are such exotic specialties as pork and clams (Portugal), paella (Spain), pork chops (Germany), cannelloni and lasagne (Italy) and curry dishes (India).

Perhaps Charlie's most sought-after recipe is the one for its

The magnificent West Hotel at 5th St., and Hennepin Ave., until razed in 1940. It was the city's best hotel for 50 years. Louis Menage lived in it as he built the first skyscraper. Everybody stayed in it from Sarah Bernhardt, etc. It is now a very dingy parking lot, but may be reclaimed. Of all of the buildings, it is the only one that most old-timers mention.

(Library of Congress)

Looking south on Nicollet Ave., in the mid-1850s from the corner of 2nd St., and Nicollet, toward Washington.

Traffic jam at 6th St., and Nicollet Ave., in 1905. Cars, horses, street-
cars, bikes and no traffic light.

potato salad. A bowl of the salad and a bowl of herring are on each table regularly at lunch.

"Women used to beg Charlie to get that recipe," Mrs. Saunders said. "He wouldn't tell. I didn't know it until I married him." It remains Charlie's best-kept secret.

Louise Saunders works hard now to maintain the image that her husband and his employees created: good food served in quiet comfort. "I think the formula for a successful restaurant starts with good food," she said. "Then there must be good service and a pleasant decor. Nothing gaudy. Quiet elegance that men like and women appreciate because it gives them a background to glow in."

She thought a minute and then added: "What is unique about restaurants in Minneapolis is that most of them continue to be home-owned. There are no good restaurant chains here. Charlie's, Harry's, Murray's, and many others are great restaurants because the people who own them really care about their customers."

That's true. There are so many excellent restaurants in Minneapolis and its suburbs, it can be difficult to decide where to go. For the record, I'll bravely list some restaurants that have never failed me—plus a few that have. Those few are included because other Minneapolitans like them.

Alphabetically, they go like this:

BECKY'S: It isn't Sardi's, but this is where the actors from the Tyrone Guthrie Theatre hang out and eat well. So do all the other

(Left) Dayton's, the major department store and as the Dayton-Hudson Corp., one of the major retailing firms in the U.S., now stands where the church is. That's the old Westminster Presbyterian at Nicollet (foreground) and 7th St. Across from that site on the right side of Nicollet today (where the tree is) is the IDS Center with its 57-story tower and Crystal Court. And Nicollet is bridged by one of the city's many 2nd story skyways. This photo was taken in 1886. Dayton's started on the corner in 1902.

people who have made Becky's a habit for years. It's a cafeteria with old-world class and home-cooked food.

BLACK FOREST INN: The food is German and so are the surroundings, but it's not for calorie-counters. Among the unforgettable items if you can get in the door are the mushrooms on toast.

CAMELOT: Host Hans Skalle wanted to serve food fit for a king, so he built a castle—complete with moat and drawbridge. It's fairy-tale-style architecture that unfortunately was plunked down right next to a freeway. Inside, however, you dine in royal splendor without traffic noise. It's a *Holiday* Magazine award winner.

CHANHASSEN FRONTIER: Herb Bloomberg, a construction man, put up a group of restaurants and theaters under one roof in a Minneapolis suburb, Chanhassen. Now he's an entrepreneur. At the dinner theater, you dine in a Las Vegas-size room and see such Broadway musicals on the big stage as *South Pacific* or *How to Succeed in Business without Really Trying*. The Downstairs Playhouse offers food with such intimate entertainment items as Dylan Thomas's *Under Milkwood* or James Thurber's *Thurber Carnival*. The food is good and the place offers fun for the whole family.

CHARLIE'S CAFE EXCEPTIONALE: What more can I say? A *Holiday* Magazine award winner for twenty-two years.

CHATEAU DE PARIS: It has tried to be as authentically French as is possible in the middle of the Upper Midwest, ever since it opened about 15 years ago. Its location in the Dyckman Hotel is close to everything, and although the management and menu has been changed, the classic Spaghetti Milanaise (Julienne ham, beef, salami and tongue, plus sauce, plus cheese, plus spaghetti) is as tasty as ever.

DAYTON'S OAK GRILL: A handsome room at the top of Dayton's department store, it caters to a big luncheon crowd daily. It is open at night only when the store is. The food is good and basically American, although they occasionally stage week-long festivals of foreign dishes. This is also one of the few spots in town where you can buy table wine by the glass to drink with your meal. In the adjoining Sky Room, the big crush at noon is caused by the salad bar where you concoct your own bowl of greenery.

Delicatessens—Minneapolis bulges with good "deli" restaurants. Downtown, don't miss The Brothers, and The Brothers Too. The big-timers in the residential area are two Lincoln "Delis"—serving spectacular matzo ball soup, among other things —and Bernie's. All of them draw crowds.

DI NAPOLI: A Hennepin Ave. landmark and one of the few good restaurants left on that street worth visiting. Italian food is what it's all about and there is good Italian wine to accompany it. What else is there?

DONALDSON'S GRILL: If your wish is for fish broiled in butter, Donaldson's, the oldest department store in Minneapolis, is famous for it. The Grill is packed at lunch and is open at night when the store is. Donaldson's also cornered the maple frango market years ago and it continues to be a traditional dessert there.

DUFF'S: Where the sports fans and players meet to josh and nosh. Joe Duffy, a handsome Irish sports enthusiast, is your host. Curiously, the head chef is a woman, the attractive Mrs. Betty Nickelson. Duff's is famous for Betty's hearty soups and all sorts of other heroic dishes. This is very good eating.

FLAME ROOM: One of the oldest hotel dining rooms in the area, the Flame Room has retained its elegance and good food. After Curtis Carlson, Minneapolis' and the world's Gold Bond trading stamp king, bought the Radisson Hotel, he introduced the Golden Strings to the room. This group of symphony violinists serenade several times nightly. Their music helps to make the Flame Room the place to celebrate romantic anniversaries.

FORUM CAFETERIA: This Minneapolis landmark surrounds diners with the "kickiest" Depression-era "art moderne" decor in town. If you loved the 1930's or think you did, eat here. The food is ample and tasty and not very expensive. The carriage trade may ignore the place, but you shouldn't.

FRANCO'S: The southern suburb of Burnsville is home to a young Swiss chef, Franco Loris. Franco was brought to Minneapolis during the fondue craze of the 1960s to head the restaurants for the Dayton's stores. After working for a couple of other employers, he is now his own boss. The food and the European atmosphere show it.

FRIAR'S DINNER THEATER: Broadway plays with your meal make this a special evening out downtown. Again, the food is good, but not great, but such well-known TV faces as Dody Goodman, Fannie Flagg and Kathy Nolan show up to star in the productions.

FUJI-YA: A GI war bride from Japan, Mrs. Reiko Weston came to Minneapolis with a dream. She wanted to own a Japanese tea house in a typical Japanese setting—under a bridge, beside a flowing stream near a waterfall. She searched and found a site on the Mississippi River downtown in the old flour-milling district. It's just across from St. Anthony Falls and under the 3rd Avenue bridge. Diners sit Japanese-style at low tables, eating the best of Japanese cuisine. The food is cooked at the table by pretty Japanese girls. Sukiyaki, teriyaki and tempura are all excellent. So is the hospitality. It's one of Minneapolis' best restaurants.

And if you don't believe·there is such a thing as a Japanese cafeteria, then a visit to Fuji-Ya International in Minneapolis' Cedar-Riverside area is a "must."

HABERDASHERY: This is a little bit of midtown Manhattan "chichi" transplanted into a former haberdashery store off the lobby of the Radisson Hotel. The management—Curtis Carlson again—suggests you throw peanut shells on the floor while nibbling peanuts with drinks. Food is in the sandwich, soup and hot dish vein, but there's variety daily and it's good. Arrive early to get a window table. The object here is to see and be seen, so the place attracts the fashionables.

HARRY'S CAFE: One of Minneapolis' oldest and best, it ranks along with Charlie's as a favorite place to go for Minneapolis residents. It regularly wins a *Holiday* Magazine honorable mention award. Harry's has had several owners since it opened in the 1930's, but its old downtown town house site continues to provide a charming background for good food. Order anything. And don't pass up the hot popovers.

HOT FISH SHOP: The original restaurant has been on the same corner in Winona, Minn., about 100 miles southeast of the Twin

Another view of Nicollet in 1900 looking from 6th toward 5th.

"It's the same Old Moon a-shining"

Cities, for 40 years. Its branch in Mendota—a historic village at the edge of the Twins—serves the same fresh walleyed pike in the identical light batter. That batter does wonders for tired onion rings, too.

ICHABOD'S WET GOODS: The young, handsome and affluent hang out here to drink, eat occasionally and be merry as all get-out with lots of spiffy contests and things. Its window tables are as much in demand as those at the Haberdashery across the street.

IDS CENTER: If you get lost anywhere in the crystal court, you won't go hungry. The Marquette Inn, the hotel that is a part of the giant complex, features three restaurants. The Crossroads bar and restaurant offers inexpensive lunches—some on a balcony overlooking the court—and dinner, plus nightly entertainment. The Gallery, on another balcony overlooking the court, is famous for its fondue dishes. The elegant, most expensive spot is the Marquis, which offers traditional continental cuisine with all of those fattening sauces. Also opening off of the court are two splendid Woolworth's eating spots, a coffee shop and a cafeteria. In the near future, there will be another IDS restaurant on the 50th floor of the 57-story Tower.

JAX CAFE: Another family-owned marvel, this was, until 1973, the only restaurant in Minneapolis with outdoor garden tables. They're for summer use, of course, but Jax is a jolly place any time of year, and the food is excellent. In summer, Jack Kozlak, the host, keeps a trout stream stocked in the garden; order trout and you can watch a pretty waitress run out and catch it for you. Non-fish fans will enjoy the crisp and crackling roast duckling.

LA CASA ORONADO: Speaking of families, don't miss Mama and Papa Coronado and all of the little Coronados—children, grandchildren, nieces, nephews and cousins. Together they operate a tasty Mexican restaurant with live Mariachi music, occasional Mexican hat dancers plus enchiladas, tostadas, chicken mole—and ice water, on request. The Coronados have been in

Early advertisement for a Pillsbury cereal. It appeared in the *Woman's Home Companion Magazine* in 1897 the restaurant business in the Twin Cities for almost fifty years, but they haven't forgotten their old Mexican recipes. The food is hot, spicy and superb.

THE LODGE: Everything on the menu is from Minnesota, from the home-grown roast turkey, pheasant, duck, goose or not-so-plain pork to the vegetables of the Jolly Green Giant. The idea to open a restaurant featuring only Minnesota foods belongs (again) to Curtis Carlson. A dinner beside the big fireplace is a great place to entertain the family. Obviously, Minnesota's famous wild rice is a staple on this menu.

LORD FLETCHER'S: It's oh-so-very English. On cold winter nights with the wind whistling across Lake Minnetonka, some expect to see Heathcliff, Sherlock Holmes and the Baskervilles' hound dog dining together on beef stew and English trifle. What you do see is snowmobilers in winter and sailors in summer. A popular lakeside spot.

MARKET BAR-B-Q: Another traditional spot, this is popular with such night-lights as entertainers, musicians and newspaper people. The ribs are the thing, and I'm corny enough to say that they are rib-tickling good. If you don't want to stay, the Market does a dandy take-out business.

MARRIOTT EXCHANGE: This tribute to the Minneapolis Grain Exchange located at the Marriott Inn is unique for a couple of reasons. The designer used authentic grain bags, barrels and carts for the decor and it shows to charming advantage. The second reason? The bright young designer is a son of entertainer Garry Moore.

MICHAEL'S OF GOLDEN VALLEY: The food is more important than the atmosphere here, although regular customers make it a clubby spot. Everything is good, but, on a hot day, the cold sea-food salad with Michael's own dressing is extra special.

MURRAY'S: The late Art Murray believed in steaks. His widow, Marie, has never stopped believing and that's why Murray's is Minneapolis' greatest steak house. The Silver Butterknife steak is the most renowned, but there are all sorts of other good things on the menu, plus such fillers as hot garlic toast and home-made desserts. Another Minneapolis institution.

NAN-KIN: The oldest Chinese restaurant in Minneapolis continues to hold its own by offering splendid Szechuan and Cantonese food. Right downtown, it serves shoppers, family parties and people who just love Chinese food. Craig Claiborne, former food editor of the New York *Times*, told me it is the best Chinese restaurant he'd found between the two coasts. Minneapolitans have known that for years.

NORMANDY KITCHEN and NORMANDY VILLAGE: These two popular restaurants are in the Normandy Hotel. The Kitchen doesn't serve liquor with its home-style food; the Village does, along with its old-English decor and charcoal-broiled specialties. Regular fillers at the Village include hot popovers, Caesar salad and a Roquefort cheese spread.

PETER'S GRILL: In 1974, Peter Atcas and his family will have been doing business near the same downtown Minneapolis corner for 60 years. The Grill is the unofficial coffee house for medical men with offices in the area. One reason is that Peter's food has always been good and his pies are spectacular. The present "art deco" style building dates from 1930.

POWERS ROLL AND BOWL: It's a sidewalk cafe on the Nicollet Mall sidewalk in summer and a cozy corner of the department store (indoors) all year around. The big feature is that you can have your sandwich made on about a dozen kinds of homemade foreign-style bread. Oh, yes, the bowl is for good soup.

PRACNA-ON-MAIN: This is the newest winner in a series of unusual restaurants owned by the Naegele family of Lord Fletcher's fame. Pracna, in a 19th-century saloon building bearing the name "Pracna" on its facade, overlooks the Mississippi river on historic Main Street that was in the original Village of St. Anthony. It is just across the river from downtown Minneapolis. The hope is that Pracna will spawn more new shops in old and curious buildings there. The food and drink is served in an outdoor garden or an indoor garden with skylight or in antique booths in the ancient basement.

THE RAINBOW: Christ Legeros came to Minneapolis from Greece a bit more than fifty years ago and opened The Rainbow. It remains the city's top family dining spot, featuring luscious

Downtown Minneapolis in 1857, the year before Minnesota became a state. Scene looks south on Washington Ave., from 2nd Ave. S.

The loop in 1900 showing in the foreground the New York Life Insurance building at 5th St., and 2nd Ave. S., looking toward Nicollet (or toward the southwest).

The Minikahda Club in 1899, the country club in the city overlooking Lake Calhoun. The Club remains one of the two most affluent and prestigious. It is one of two golf and country clubs that one can get to via public bus.

This photo is taken from about the site of the Walker Art Center looking toward Minneapolis skyline of 1874. The lake in the foreground is still there in Loring Park. It was then known as Johnson's lake, then Central Park lake, until named after park benefactor, A. C. Loring. The house belongs to H. W. Welles, first mayor of the Village of St. Anthony. The Welles house stands where the Episcopal Cathedral of St. Mark stands today, across from Walker Art Center, and Loring Park. There are still relatives of Walker and Welles families prominent in civic affairs. The house stands at a crossroads of Hennepin and Lyndale Aves., known as the Bottleneck. The two streets evolved from two Indian paths.

fried chicken, roast pork with dressing as good as Granny's used to be, and superlative home-made soups—lentil, pea, bean, chicken, vegetable, anything. Christ is still around—particularly in the morning, when freshly-baked bread is a popular breakfast item—but the usual hosts are his handsome sons, George and John. Since they've produced grandsons for Christ, let's hope The Rainbow never fades away. It's the best.

DUDLEY RIGGS' BRAVE NEW WORKSHOP ALSO: Riggs, a juvenile circus aerialist who grew up to open Minneapolis' first coffee house, runs two spots now. Both offer satirical reviews and improvisational theater, but only the Also features Riggs' famous homemade soups, unusual breads and fattening hazelnut torte. For lunch, dinner or after-the-show supper, it's a favorite.

ROSEWOOD ROOM: Here is continental dining beside a glistening swimming pool seven stories up—just off the lobby of the unique Northstar Inn, one of Minneapolis' newest hotels, built above its own six-story parking ramp. The menu includes entire gourmet-style dinners from Europe to Asia, and the wine list is excellent. A *Holiday* Magazine award winner.

RUSCIANO'S: Frank Rusciano serves the best lasagna in town. This restaurant has bloomed from behind the Italian grocery store he used to operate downtown. Now he's in the restaurant business only. He has courageously catered through the years to the newspaper crowd. Others who like it there are grain brokers from the nearby Minneapolis Grain Exchange and the gang from city hall. Everybody is a *paisan* of Frank Rusciano.

SHERATON-RITZ: Minneapolis' most elegantly decorated downtown hotel offers diners two restaurants. There is the old English Cheshire Cheese, the French Brasserie and up in the penthouse, a bar named Sadie's Parlor. In pleasant weather, diners can eat outdoors beside the swimming pool. The entire layout is worth a look and a linger because it is one of the gems in Minneapolis' lower loop urban renewal area.

TAJ MAHAL: A restaurant featuring the foods of India in the middle of downtown Minneapolis. It can be as curried and as unhurried as you want it to be.

Tea Rooms—Only three qualifiers are left in the running.

Loretta's, about five minutes from downtown in a handsome apartment building, is excellent and fattening. Five-Ten Groveland, also in an elegant apartment building about five minutes from downtown, is too. Downtown, the last of the old-fashioned and excellent department store tea rooms is at Young-Quinlan's on the Nicollet Mall. Y-Q, however, serves liquor with its cheese souffles and pecan rolls.

TIFFANY: Fine French-style food (FFF) in a breathtaking setting of original Tiffany glass lamps and chandeliers. The restaurant is the idea (again) of Curtis Carlson and it's located in his suburban Radisson South hotel. (Also on the premises is the Shipside, a restaurant featuring an oyster bar.)

WAIKIKI ROOM: This Polynesian room off the lobby of the historic Pick-Nicollet Hotel downtown is one of the city's unsung best restaurants. Indian curries, Cantonese and American dishes are available, along with the shark fins and ukelele music. Perfect for a romantic or rousing luau.

WALKER ART CENTER CAFETERIA: It is the only open-air, roof-top, sculpture-court dining in town, and superb. Not just the atmosphere, but the food. Although it's served cafeteria-style, the menu is wonderfully cosmopolitan with emphasis on Scandinavian-style open-face sandwiches and all-American strawberry pie or chocolate or banana cream. Don't miss it.

EDDIE WEBSTER PUB-ON-THE-MALL: Not only is the pub the first to open a sidewalk cafe on the Nicollet Mall, but the restaurant is also the first to be built inside the helix of a parking ramp. It makes for a circular marvel of a spot on three levels. More important, though, is that the food is excellent (as it is at Eddie Webster's suburban location near the Bloomington sports complex). A warning, though, to dieters. Eddie's diet special—top ground sirloin—is accompanied by two slices of super sourdough bread drenched in butter.

WIG AND BOTTLE: Gourmets who know insist that the W and B owns the finest wine cellar in town. The food is truly of the gourmet variety, too, with special events, such as a golden goose dinner, that draw crowds.

WINE CELLAR: Short on tables and long on its wine list, the

Looking from the east bank of the Mississippi (which was St. Anthony Village until 1872) across to the city of Minneapolis on the west bank. This picture was taken in 1870 from the Winslow House Hotel. At right is the second suspension bridge at Hennepin Ave. In the foreground is the downriver tip of Nicollet island and a log jam.

(Left above) Once again, Hennepin Ave., and the Pence opera house with the Mississippi river in background just a block away. 1869.

(Left below) Scene in 1870 on Washington Ave., between Nicollet Ave., and Marquette, just before beginning of Northern Pacific RR construction out west. An exploring expedition into the Dakota country to determine route started from Minneapolis. This photo shows some of the covered wagons, etc.

The Union Block on Hennepin Ave., at Bridge Square in 1869.

(Left above) City skyline with Foshay Tower in 1940s. At 32 stories it was the skyline's dominant silhouette from 1929 until IDS Tower opened in 1972.

(Left below) This is a great photo of Minneapolis, from Winslow House. Dated 1876. Shows a better view of the Hennepin Ave. suspension bridge across the river's main channel.

The Academy of Music at Hennepin and Washington—across Hennepin from old Nicollet Hotel—in the 1860s.

Powers Dry Goods Co., on Nicollet at 5th St. about 1905. Powers is still there.

Wine Cellar is a small restaurant for true gourmets. Located off the seventh-floor lobby of the Northstar Inn, it is open to the public for dinner only. At noon it is a private club for big eaters. The food, usually a different one-dinner-only menu each night, is always excellent. Plan not to hurry here. Dining takes time, and the waiters don't like it if you rush away before the souffle.

WHITE HOUSE: Irv Schechtman opened a Cantonese restaurant some years ago and did well. Then he added a San Francisco decor to a part of his place and imported a chef to do Italian food San Francisco-style. Today diners can enjoy either a Cantonese or Italian menu with many other Continental dishes. Everything tastes good and nobody goes away hungry.

HOWARD WONG'S: The Chinese Wong family came from the Dakotas to Minnesota and it's our gain. They set an exotic table at this big, new and hospitable restaurant that is a perfect spot to lunch or dine before any sports event in Bloomington.

There are two famous restaurants within a short drive of downtown Minneapolis that should be on the list of all visitors. Both are *Holiday* award winners.

At Stillwater, Minnesota, on the St. Croix River about an hour's drive from Minneapolis, is the Lowell Inn. It's a hotel and restaurant that was created by the late Nelle Palmer, grande dame of area restaurateurs. The Lowell Inn offers wonderful all-American cooking and homemade pastries in its main dining rooms. The Matterhorn Room features continental food and lots of fondue. Don't miss it.

At Hastings, Minnesota, where the St. Croix river meets the Mississippi, the Mississippi Belle restaurant blossoms. Until 1972, Mrs. Audrey Reissner was in charge of all the good food. Fortunately for her devotees, Mrs. Reissner left her recipes behind when she retired. The background is a replica of an old river steamboat salon recreated in one of the nineteenth-century buildings on Main Street. Chicken, steak, lobster, everything cooked by Audrey's crew, is excellent because they use her unusual recipes. Audrey's soups—dill pickle, peanut butter and cucumber bisque—are not to be missed. Specialties include hot homemade orange rolls and Audrey's cream pies.

No record of Minneapolis' fine restaurants would be complete without a word about a calorically historic site that is no more—Richards Treat. The cafeteria operated for many years by Lenore Richards and Nola Treat was a landmark for great home cooking served cafeteria style. It attracted everybody who was anybody and a lot of people who just became addicted to their ham loaf, Wellesley fudge cake, rhubarb pie and other glorious dishes. Miss Richards and Miss Treat, both home economists, not only operated the restaurant, but they also wrote the definitive textbook on cooking in quantity.

When their building was to be razed for the new First National Bank building, they decided to retire. Nobody has replaced them downtown, and they are definitely missed. All of us who loved Richards Treat are sadder, but slimmer.

But cooking is not the only fine art practiced in town. Minneapolis set out to "get cultured" fast and early. That yearning to learn from the arts was already at work in 1856 when Ole Bull, an intrepid violinist from Norway, drew standing-room-only crowds to his concerts.

Although Ole Bull was among the first imported artists to visit the city, there were singing societies in good voice there even before Minneapolis was chartered. The Swedes, Norwegians, Danes, Germans and the Congregationalists, Episcopalians and Baptists were all involved in early-day choral groups. Many of those choral clubs survive today. The most famous is the mighty all-male Apollo Club chorus. Apollo Club performances continue to draw crowds even after seventy-five years.

For the official record, Minneapolis today boasts a top-ranked symphony orchestra, two major art museums plus the charming American-Swedish Institute, the well-established Old Log Theater, the internationally-famous Tyrone Guthrie Theatre and all sorts of growing cultural "babies." They include the Minnesota Opera Company, several dance companies, dozens of smaller music groups and all sorts of little theaters.

The Old Log, an Equity stock company located in nearby Excelsior, has survived twenty-five seasons, first as a "straw hat" summer venture and nowadays on a year-round basis. Audiences regularly thank Don Stolz, who has been producer and director of the Old Log through the years. Another theater company of note is Theater-in-the-Round, a semiprofessional organization with an international reputation. Their open auditions attract both professional actors and budding amateurs.

Newest addition to the cultural scene is the Children's Theatre Company at the Minneapolis Institute of Arts. Under its director, John Donahue, it has been artistically mature enough to attract national praise and a $250,000 grant from the Rockefeller Foundation.

Oddly enough, the University of Minnesota does not provide the cultural clout in the community that might be expected from such a mighty institution. While the University Theater swings, winter and summer, (its old-time Showboat Theater on the Mississippi river is a summertime must), the University's art gallery with a splendid collection of early twentieth-century paintings and sculpture has been almost hidden from the public in the "attic" of Northrop Auditorium for forty years. The most gala season of culture on the campus is when the Metropolitan Opera Company of New York plays a week at Northrop every spring.

In 1879, Minneapolis had its first art museum. Thomas Barlow Walker, a lumberman, opened a room in his home to anybody who wanted to view the art he began collecting in 1874. Walker's house stood on a corner downtown by a trolley stop. His gallery usually was well-attended, particularly on cold winter days.

By 1883, a new organization, the Minneapolis Society of Fine Arts, opened art classes in the public library and had its first art exhibit. A newspaper article of the day was cordial to the display, which included an antique fireman's bucket, a Norwegian beer can, a portrait of George Washington by Rembrandt Peale, a cane made from the chimney piece in William Penn's house and some vases loaned by the Pillsbury family.

At the Art Institute, Minneapolis' public museum, nothing is left from that first art exhibition of 1883 staged by the Minneapolis Society of Fine Arts. The Society's board of trustees

Looking down at the busy corner (today) of 7th St., and Hennepin Ave., in the heart of the movie, theater and bar district—as it was in 1905. Tower building at left is the old Jefferson School. In the background is an area where a new downtown major league football stadium (domed) for the Minnesota Vikings is planned. Picture was taken from top of Radisson Hotel, which still stands on 7th St., and is one of city's finest.

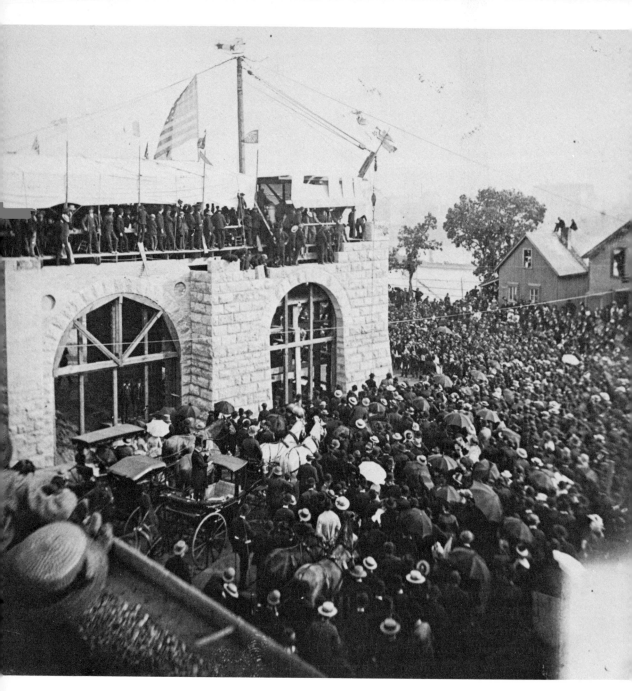

Cornerstone ceremony in May, 1886 for new Exposition building, on site of Winslow House. Building cost $250,000. It was opened to public in August, 1886.

An 1857 view of the business district—looking north from 2nd Ave. S., and 4th St. In center background are pillars for the first Hennepin Ave. suspension bridge across the river. They were wooden towers. The second bridge towers were stone.

Looking upriver toward the city of Minneapolis from about 10th Ave. S. (today). This is an 1869 photo. Logs are floating in foreground.

today is the governing body for the Institute, the Children's theatre and the Minneapolis College of Art and Design. In place of the Norwegian beer can and the antique fireman's bucket is a magnificent art collection ranging historically from ancient Greece and China to modern Manhattan.

The "Lucretia" painting by Rembrandt is among the major works on view along with a great Manet, "The Smoker," a splendid El Greco, "Christ Driving the Money Changers from the Temple," a spectacular Max Beckmann triptych, "Blindman's Buff," and a bizarre Tom Wesselman, "Mouth #10."

Sculpture, period rooms, a treasure of Chinese bronzes given by the late Alfred F. Pillsbury, and a rare silver tea service by Paul Revere, plus drawings, prints and photographs are in the Institute's fine permanent collection. Today the museum needs more room to expand. When the present building by the architectural firm of McKim, Meade and White opened in 1915, only a few works of art were on view.

The museum was built with funds raised in Minneapolis on land that was once the rose garden of Mrs. Dorilus Morrison, wife of Minneapolis' first mayor. Dorilus' son, Clinton Morrison, gave the land to start the fund campaign.

It is important to note that opening night at the museum may have been one of the earlier hands-across-the-river ventures between Minneapolis and St. Paul. The new museum was so grand and so empty that the trustees asked for a loan of some art from a well-known St. Paul collector, James J. Hill. Hill was delighted to cooperate, and a horse and wagon was sent across the river to pick up his art objects and carry them to Minneapolis. He even attended the reception to see how his things looked.

The man who did the most to build a collection for the Institute was Russell Plimpton of Palm Beach, Florida. Plimpton was the Institute's director for thirty-five years from 1921 until his retirement in 1956. It was Plimpton who found the Paul Revere tea service and together with another devoted Minneapolitan, brought it to the city. The set was purchased and given to the museum by the late Mr. and Mrs. James Ford Bell. Bell was the chief executive of General Mills. His son, Charles, now chairman emeritus of the firm, succeeded his father in devotion to the museum. Bell is a long-time trustee of the Society and served as chairman of the board of trustees. (His younger brother, Samuel, is an artist. The oldest, James Ford Bell Jr., known as Ford Bell, is the family maverick. Not only did he refuse to work for his father at General Mills, but he founded his own successful retail food business and actively supported Democratic candidates in political campaigns. Ford, who made his first movie 40 years ago, recently completed writing, directing and producing a second film with professional actors in major roles.)

"Many of the people who supported us in those earlier days," Plimpton said, "were not collectors, and some were not even particularly knowledgeable in the arts.

"But they were typical Minneapolitans. By that I mean that they felt the responsibility to give financial support to their cultural institutions and they always did it to the best of their means."

Clinton Morrison, Minneapolis bank executive, recently stepped down as chairman of the Society's trustees. He is a great-grandson of Dorilus and a grandson and namesake of Clinton. As a fourth-generation supporter of the Society, the museum and the college, he had to face up to a new era in fund-raising to meet the cultural explosion.

In 1972, the trustees engaged Kenzo Tange, one of Japan's major architects, to enlarge and renew the fifty-eight-year-old Institute building and to design a stunning new series of buildings for the college. In making his plans, Tange was alerted by the trustees that the Institute and the Children's Theatre must become more open to the public than ever before.

"There was a time," said Morrison, "when museums, at least in this country, although public institutions, were considered to be quite precious.

"Now we know more than ever that a museum must reach out and truly be a part of the life of the community. This does not mean that quality and taste would be less emphasized. It is just that the role of a museum today is no longer that of bringing enjoyment to only a few erudite patrons and collectors. It must bring enjoyment and excitement to the total community and through examples of the best of the past try to stimulate creativity in the present."

So the future of the ninety-year-old Society, its eighty-seven-year-old college and its fifty-eight-year-old museum looks optimistic. All Minneapolis has to do is raise the money. It is inevitable that Minneapolis will, simply because it always has.

That doesn't mean that Minneapolis culture supporters turn down outside funds. It is just that when Minneapolitans begin a fund drive for anything, they are prepared to raise most of the money among themselves.

The story of the Minnesota Orchestra is a good illustration of that. Since that first concert in 1903, concert audiences have continued to grow. During a typical season, the ninety-eight member orchestra, conducted by Stanislaw Skrowaczewski, an energetic and dashing native of Poland, plays to over 600,000 listeners. This includes regular Thursday, Friday and Sunday concerts, plus extra appearances in and out of the Twin Cities. Box office receipts can't pay all the bills, however. That's why the board of the Minnesota Orchestral Association and the 2,000-member Women's Association of the Minnesota Orchestra, (WAMSO), continually look for new ways to raise money.

In recent years, the board raised more than $10,000,000 with its New Dimensions Fund drive. The campaign was held in addition to the annual Guaranty Fund drive. One part of the New Dimensions Fund was a program urging the endowment of special orchestral "chairs." To date, 13 donors have given $250,000 each to the project. The chair of the orchestra's concertmaster was endowed in memory of Elbert L. Carpenter, Minneapolis lumberman who originally organized the orchestra 70 years ago.

As for the women of WAMSO, their biggest fund-raiser continues to be an annual symphony ball. In 1970, for example, a silent auction of written bids only at the ball raised $71,595 for the orchestra. Actor Danny Kaye conducted the orchestra before

Minnehaha Creek.

The Rose Fete, an annual festival at Minneapolis Institute of Arts.

At left, one of two buildings of the Towers apartments (where I live, by the way) and in the foreground is the Yamasaki building for John Pillsbury's Northwestern National Life Insurance Co. Both stand on the site of Bridge Square, original city center where Hennepin and Nicollet Aves. met. In other words, we are practically across the street from where John Stevens and the boys met to name Minneapolis. The Mississippi is 1-1/2 blocks to the left.

Largest ethnic festival—Svenskarnas Dag (Swedish Day)—attracts 40,000 or so to Minnehaha Park.

Martin Friedman, director of Walker Art Center, on sculpture terrace with view of city skyline behind him. Foshay Tower is the major building shown.

the ball in 1973. The concert and ball together raised $114,000 for the orchestra.

The complete history of the orchestra was told by the late John K. Sherman, former Minneapolis Star arts critic, in his book, *Music and Maestros*. In it, Sherman traced the orchestra's growth through its conductors—Emil Oberhoffer, Henri Verbrugghen, Eugene Ormandy, Dimitri Mitropoulos and Antal Dorati, Skrowaczewski's immediate predecessor.

Recently, Ormandy, the renowned maestro of the Philadelphia Orchestra, reshuffled some of his personal memories for me.

Ormandy was just thirty years old in 1931 when he took over the podium of the then Minneapolis Symphony from Verbrugghen. "I still remember very well my first concert," Ormandy told me. "The Minneapolis audience was just marvelous to me. The house was completely sold out. And right from the stage it was announced that there would be another concert Sunday afternoon. That was the first of the Sunday afternoon concerts. From Friday night until Sunday afternoon, the house was sold out again."

On that first night in Northrop Auditorium, a barny hall with 4,800 seats and accoustics so bad that it is maddening to both musicians and the audience, Ormandy said he really didn't know where he was. "I knew it was a big auditorium and the orchestra and the audience were responding to me," he said.

The old story in town is that Ormandy hated that hall. It is told that once, when a reporter asked him what should be used to improve Northrop's accoustics, Ormandy replied, "Dynamite."

Ormandy laughed and said, "Whether I made a remark like that or not—and it does sound like me—I don't remember. You know, I was forty years younger then.

"And I was a conductor who believed that the Minneapolis orchestra could become a second Philadelphia orchestra in two years. I had this desire.

(Left) In summer, same guys exchange snowmobiles for boats.

"What I didn't know then was that Northrop was built to be a lecture hall. When I was back there again a couple of years ago, I still considered it a lecture hall.

"Skrowaczewski is a good friend of mine by the way. He is very good. Treat him well and give him everything he asks—especially a good concert hall."

In 1973, the board heeded Ormandy's words. In yet another fund campaign, board members raised $6.6 million to build a new concert hall in Minneapolis. It is located one block from the present end of the Nicollet Mall on the site of the old Minneapolis Auditorium where the orchestra first played. The auditorium building was renamed the Lyceum Theater. In recent years, the theater was an evangelistic temple. The new hall is scheduled to open for the orchestra's 1974-75 season.

Looking back again, Ormandy credited Minneapolis and its orchestra "for giving me my big chance in life."

"I did not sit on a high horse as some conductors like to do," he said. "I worked with the musicians and I was their friend and one of them. I still feel that way in Philadelphia with our orchestra. We worked together beautifully in Minneapolis. And we had such wonderful crowds—even, you know, in the coldest of winters.

"The weather in Minneapolis has been there long before the concerts," Ormandy commented. "The people have always accepted that. I remember when I conducted, I would drive over two or three inches of snow and ice to the concert hall and never give it a thought. The weather in winter became a challenge to me and to the audiences. I think Minneapolis is lucky to have so many culturally inspired people."

Ormandy also paid tribute to the Minneapolis citizens who served on the orchestra's board of directors. "The board was always headed by dedicated men beginning with the late Elbert L. Carpenter." Ormandy called Carpenter "my Minneapolis stepfather."

It was Carpenter, a transplanted Iowa native and head of a major lumber company in Minneapolis, who got twenty-four music-lovers together and organized the first board. His son, Leonard J. Carpenter, a good friend of Ormandy's, continues to serve as a director of the orchestra.

"Your board of directors fights for the orchestra," Ormandy said. "Many of them have given money to save it in times of need. You reached the $10,000,000 mark in Minneapolis long before we did in Philadelphia, and Philadelphia is a very culturally-minded city."

Ormandy even had fond recollections of the orchestra's early concert tours. "They were eight-week tours by train in those days," he said, "and I think I was the only member of the group who was allowed to get off occasionally and take a shower at the local YMCA."

Sherman, in his book, credited Ormandy with making the Minneapolis orchestra come alive for the first time. Ormandy, to me, said it was the Minneapolis audiences who helped generate the electricity to make the concerts exciting.

"Yes, I fell in love with Minneapolis the minute I arrived," he said. "I still call it my first love."

Skrowaczewski has been conductor of the orchestra now for more than ten years, and has had continued support, just as Ormandy had at the box-office and behind the scenes.

Minneapolis has its second major art museum, the Walker Art Center, because of a misunderstanding that happened more than sixty years ago. By 1912, when the Minneapolis Society of Fine Arts decided to build the Minneapolis Institute of Arts, Thomas Barlow Walker had acquired quite a variety of art for his at-home gallery. Walker was delighted with the Institute plan and was ready to give his entire collection to the museum. Now, some of it was splendid—works by David, Corot and Courbet, for example. But some of it didn't meet standards set by the new Institute's art experts.

Walker, so the story goes, decided that if the Institute wouldn't take all of his collection, it wouldn't get any of it. That's when he decided to build his own museum. He picked a site for it on Lowry Hill overlooking Loring Park. It was dedicated in 1927

The late Archie Walker Sr., son of T. B. Walker, who established the private Walker gallery in his home in 1879. Archie Walker was instrumental in helping the Guthrie Theater get started by offering land adjacent to the Walker Art Center for it. He died in 1972.

The opening of the Walker Art Center in 1971.

with Walker on hand to greet visitors, just as he always did when his home-grown gallery was a favorite place to wait for the street-cars.

Through the years, the Walker family has kept the museum open free to the public, although it is operated by a private family foundation. Since tastes do change, T.B. Walker's art collection changed with it. One influence came from one of Walker's grandsons, Hudson Walker.

Hudson set up the University of Minnesota gallery in the early 1930's and also operated a gallery in New York. He liked the modern artists of the early twentieth century—Marsden Hartley, Alfred Maurer, Stuart Davis, Ben Shahn, John Marin and many others.

Whether it was Hudson Walker's taste and knowledge that directed it or not, sometime in the last thirty-five years, the collection at the Walker began to reflect the contemporary. In the 1960's, under director H. Harvard Arnason and then Martin Friedman, the current director, the Walker became the foremost modern museum in the United States, second only to New York's Museum of Modern Art.

Such major new shows as those of contemporary British artists, South American artists, the art of Africa and others originated at the Walker.

In addition, the Walker staff was getting involved in the areas of urban design and planning, transit problems and modern living. An example was Walker's two-day program in which sculptors, painters, urban planners, architects and designers came to Minneapolis to look over and lead discussions on what to do to revitalize downtown Hennepin Avenue.

That program was only one way in which Walker gets involved in the city. It was the Walker family foundation that led the way

(Left) Lake Harriet, in the center of Minneapolis' chain of natural lakes, has a water area of 353 acres and a shoreline of 2.68 miles. It was named after wife of early Ft. Snelling commandant.

toward the building of the Tyrone Guthrie Theatre, by its grant of funds and land.

The fact that people have fun at the Walker Art Center is another reason for its popularity. Its most spectacular arty party came just before the original museum building was to be razed for the new one; party-goers were allowed to paint the halls with graffiti and graphics and even take a whack at the building with sledge hammers.

The new and second Walker Art Center building, designed by Edward L. Barnes of New York, opened on the original site in May of 1971. Built of plum-colored brick and glass, it is as contemporary in design as the art collection that's in it.

During its construction, Walker again benefited Minneapolitans by distributing its larger pieces of sculpture around town: a Lipschitz on the First National Bank Plaza, a Tony Smith on the plaza of the Northern States Power Co., and so on.

The "holes" left after Walker rounded up the sculptures for the new building may yet be refilled. Even conservative business-men grew fond of the sculptures and saw the need to add art to the cityscape.

Minneapolis' smallest art museum is the unique American-Swedish Institute. It is housed in the thirty-three-room "castle" that Swan Turnblad, a Swedish immigrant who made good, built in 1903. Turnblad spent very little time living in his turreted mansion. He gave it to Minneapolis' Swedish-American citizens some forty years ago. They have built it into an enchanting museum featuring historic exhibits, crafts, glass, paintings and sculpture. Among its delights are handsome antique porcelain stoves (Turnblad bought the best from the old country) and a magnificent Great Hall paneled in hand-carved mahogany.

There should be an historic plaque on the jazzy glass facade of the Guthrie Theater in Minneapolis reading:

"Sir Tyrone Guthrie settled (for) here."

Guthrie, always an innovator, became a kind of theatrical pioneer looking for a promising land. At the time, Broadway bored him. He said so, often and emphatically. He believed that a regional theater company of Guthrie quality could survive in the United States somewhere between the Hudson River and the Hollywood hills.

What Guthrie didn't know when he picked Minneapolis for his theater in 1960 is that it had traditionally been a town of theatergoers. The only reason that Minneapolitans were not going to the theater in the second half of the twentieth century is that there wasn't as much of the lively and legitimate available as there used to be. Downtown Hennepin Avenue and its cross streets housed a little bit of Broadway from the 1860's to the 1930's. The city was also the spawning place for a number of major entertainment personalities: Lew Ayres, Gail Sondergaard, Ann Sothern, Richard Carlson, Robert Vaughn, Arlene Dahl, the Arness (Aurness) brothers (James Arness and Peter Graves), Hilda Simms, June Hawkins and the singing Andrews sisters.

The late Judy Garland, although born in Grand Rapids, Minnesota, came back to sing at the state centennial observance in Minneapolis in 1958. Minneapolis is where Eddie Heimberger, better known today as Eddie Albert, used to deliver newspapers. And Avrom Hirsch Goldbogen, who became the remarkable Mike Todd, sold papers on downtown Minneapolis streetcorners.

Minneapolis was also a jumping-off place for many non-natives who first came to fame in its theaters and nightclubs. When the popular Bainbridge Stock Company dominated downtown 7th Street—successful for thirty years—such stars as Victor Jory, Gladys George, Alice Brady, Blanche Yurka, Marjorie Rambeau, Edith Taliaferro, Florence Reed and Marie Gale Bainbridge were among the players.

A.G. (Buzz) Bainbridge, the producer-director, was such a favorite that Minneapolis elected him mayor. Bainbridge died in 1936 before his second term in city hall, and although the stock company died with him, his widow, Marie Gale Bainbridge went on to act in Broadway plays and on television until her death.

One of her biggest opening nights came in 1957, when the old Shubert Theater, once the home of the Bainbridge company, housed the world premiere of Mike Todd's movie, *Around the World in 80 Days*.

For the event, the theater was renamed the Academy and Todd gave a dinner on stage before the show in honor of Mrs. Bainbridge. In his toast to her, Todd said, "When I was a kid in this town, I 'snuck' into this theater many times to see Marie Gale Bainbridge act. Tonight I'm finally on stage with her. I guess it's better to be lucky than smart." It was Todd's last visit to his old hometown. A year later he died in a plane crash.

By 1960, then, live theater for most Minneapolitans was only a pleasant memory. Only doughty Don Stolz was regularly offering audiences legitimate plays by a professional company at the Old Log.

At the University of Minnesota, Dr. Frank Whiting, director of the University Theater, was also drawing audiences to his campus productions, but he believed that there was room for another professional theater in town. So when he read in *Variety* that Sir Tyrone Guthrie was looking for a regional theater site, Whiting moved fast, writing Guthrie a letter inviting him to take a look at Minneapolis.

At about the same time, John Cowles Jr., who had then just succeeded his father as editor of the Minneapolis *Star* and the Minneapolis *Tribune*, met Oliver Rea at a party in Des Moines, Iowa. Rea had several successes as a Broadway producer, including a version of *Medea* with Judith Anderson. The two men talked about the theater in general and a repertory theater in particular. The next day on a train en route to the Iowa-Minnesota football game, the two men met again.

"I took pains to sit beside Oliver Rea on the train," Cowles recalled. "It was then I learned that he and Dr. Guthrie would shortly be visiting Minneapolis in response to an invitation from Dr. Whiting."

(Right) A chilly day in old Minneapolis town—Nicollet Mall sidewalks are heated so that snow melts instantly.

Technically, I can't explain this, but note that the street area of the Mall has fresh snow on it. The two women are standing in one of the heated bus shelters—heated from overhead by lamp-type fixtures—and note that the sidewalks are steaming and basically snow-free. In a heavy snow, it can pile up fast even with heated sidewalks, but my guess is that the street snow would be gone by the next morn if snow stopped.

Children wading in Minnehaha Creek.

Cowles liked Rea and he liked the idea, and he offered then to give a lunch for Rea and Guthrie when they got to town. At that time, Rea and Guthrie hoped that their theater could be located on a campus. In several of the other cities they visited, however, the welcome they received from University theater personnel had not been too warm. Whiting, on the contrary, was most enthusiastic. He definitely wanted to find a spot on the Minnesota campus for Guthrie's theater project.

"That winter," Cowles said, "it became apparent that an on-campus home for such a new repertory theater was not a very exciting thought for anybody except a few members of the university faculty."

Whiting was a good sport about it. If he couldn't have the theater on campus, he wanted it somewhere close by. Cowles set out to interest sponsors. He spoke to H. Harvard Arnason, director of the Walker Art Center. Arnason's response, Cowles said, was "immediate and enthusiastic." It was Arnason who turned Cowles toward the children and grandchildren of T.B. Walker.

The directors of the Walker Art Center wanted to add a small auditorium to the museum. Cowles and Arnason made the pitch to the directors and also the trustees of the T.B. Walker Foundation, financial parent of Walker Art Center. Their bold suggestion was that the Walker group might start a trend if they contributed the land adjacent to the museum and $400,000 toward a new Guthrie theater, that could be used by the Art Center.

The Walker directors and the Walker family liked the idea. On Memorial Day in 1960, Guthrie, Rea and their associate, Peter Zeisler, announced their decision to settle down in Minneapolis.

At the same time, the late Archie D. Walker Sr., T. B. Walker's son, made known the Walker contribution. He added that the contribution was voted on the condition that $900,000 could be raised by public solicitation during the next year.

That's when Cowles and his committee of young businessmen

(Left) Great view of old Pillsbury "A" mill from the Mississippi River. Below the mill is one of the old sluiceways.

went to work. Looking back today, Cowles admits that just the thought of trying to raise $900,000 was a wild one, even though Minneapolis had a long history of giving in support of culture.

In all, Cowles and his crew raised 2.3 million dollars—most of it from within the community.

"I actually had three large pledges in hand when I went in to talk to the Walker trustees," Cowles said. These included generous grants from the Daytons, the Minneapolis *Star* and *Tribune* Company, and the Atherton Bean family.

Bean, a Rhodes scholar, is former board chairman of International Multi-foods (formerly International Milling Co. of Minneapolis). He had long been a supporter of the Art Institute and the orchestra. And he believed as Cowles did that Minneapolis needed a first-rate theater. After these major gifts were announced, other pledges were easier to get. Money came in from throughout Minnesota. Schoolchildren even took up collections to add to the fund.

"Raising the money was really only fifty per cent of the job," Cowles said. "Visualizing the theater and converting our dream into specific proposals was just as important." That part of the job belonged primarily to Guthrie, Rea and Zeisler, with Cowles and the steering committee joining in when needed.

One obscure bit of trivia about Sir Tyrone Guthrie that many Minneapolitans soon learned was that the man rarely wore socks. He went sockless even in winter, and he knew what a Minneapolis winter could be like. Writing about his first arrival in Minneapolis in his book about the theater entitled, *A New Theatre*, Guthrie said: "Another hour in another plane brought us to Minneapolis. Here the temperature was not zero but thirty degrees below zero, and the snow was thrice as deep. The wind at Chicago screamed and whistled. At Minneapolis it was silent, but you felt that a sharp, bright sword had pierced your bowels through and through."

(Perhaps he really didn't worry too much because originally the Guthrie Theatre was to operate only in the summer. The winter seasons came along later.)

Ralph Rapson, director of the School of Architecture at the

University of Minnesota, was selected to design the theater. It took the best part of two years to build it. With its thrust stage and 1,437 in-the-round seats, the interior resembled the theater in Stratford, Ontario, Canada, which was designed at Guthrie's bidding by his costume wizard, Tanya Moiseiwitsch.

Meanwhile, the city prepared to become a theatrical mecca. After all, wasn't the greatest director of the English-speaking theater likely to attract stars from everywhere? And who cared if Broadway didn't know where Minneapolis was? The Minneapolis Chamber of Commerce would work on that.

Actually, Guthrie's idea was not to make his theater a showplace for established stars. He wanted to form a repertory company of good actors who would become a part of the Minneapolis scene on stage and off.

The stars did besiege him, though. One good actor, well-known for light comedy roles, begged Guthrie for a chance to play Shakespeare in Minneapolis. Guthrie said no. Another famous movie star offered his services and was rejected. There were probably others. Guthrie remained modest about it and wouldn't say.

He did say plenty, however, about how difficult the casting for the company was going to be, because "the American actor knows so little and cares so little about his voice. His speech is slovenly and raucous. The public, I think, would far better have it natural and accomplished."

Guthrie also believed that English and Canadian actors were more willing to take a chance on a new theater venture. "They'll take a risky, low-paid job," he said, "for the roles they get to play, while Americans are quite conventional and stick in the Broadway groove."

This was not true of all American actors, however. George Grizzard, a young American leading man or villain in the theater, movies and TV, auditioned for Guthrie and was accepted; he was almost in shock when Guthrie cast him for the title role in Shakespeare's *Hamlet*. Grizzard still likes to talk about it and claims that being directed by Guthrie remains the greatest experience of his life.

Other well-known professionals—Lee Richardson, Ed Flanders, Rita Gam, Ellen Geer, Robert Pastene, Ken Ruta, Ruth Nelson and John Cromwell—joined the company for the first season, as did two well-established stars, Hume Cronyn and his wife, Jessica Tandy. And there was Guthrie's Australian surprise, Zoe Caldwell.

Miss Caldwell won so many hearts that by mid-season of the first year, Minnesotans were referring to her as "Our Zoe," just as the Aussies did in her native land.

Tuesday, May 8, 1963, was hot in Minneapolis. Some first-nighters on that opening night held picnics in the park across the street from the theater. It's that kind of thing that makes a gala occasion in Minneapolis typically folksy.

The opening production of the Minnesota Theatre Company in the new Tyrone Guthrie Theater was *Hamlet*, with Grizzard in the leading role and Miss Tandy as his mother, Queen Gertrude. It was colorful and controversial and therefore totally Tyrone Guthrie. And it definitely sold tickets, even though Walter Kerr, the New York *Times* drama critic, called it Shakespeare in the "circus-on-a-clothesline" spirit.

It was on the second night that local theater-goers learned how a repertory theater company worked. Hume Cronyn starred in Douglas Campbell's production of Moliere's *The Miser*. Playing a small role was Grizzard, the *Hamlet* of opening night.

The Miser also introduced Miss Caldwell and Miss Gam to the audiences. They both scored again with Miss Tandy in Guthrie's production of *The Three Sisters* by Chekhov. Cronyn and Miss Tandy rounded out the repertory by playing the leading roles in Arthur Miller's *Death of a Salesman*.

It was a good first season. In fact, all the seasons at the Guthrie have been more good than bad, although audiences did quibble about some of the dramatic choices offered.

They didn't complain about the hit of the second season, however. It was George Bernard Shaw's *St. Joan*. Ellen Geer played the title role. When a member of the cast needed to produce a Welsh accent for his role, Guthrie reached out into the com-

It's a great place for kids!

Young fishermen at Lake Harriet.

In Minnehaha Creek.

munity to nab the dean of the Episcopal Cathedral Church of St. Mark for the coaching job. The Very Reverend Henry N. Hancock was born in Wales, and although he spoke English beautifully enough to suit Guthrie, he also remembered the speech of his native country.

Guthrie regularly attended St. Mark's during his years as a Minneapolis resident because he liked to listen to Dean Hancock. Guthrie also liked to sing hymns, and he did so in a red-blooded baritone voice that gave confidence to the more timid parishioners in the crowd. Dean Hancock, a true Welshman, was in favor of lusty hymn-singing. He was delighted whenever Guthrie showed up and sang out.

When Guthrie first came to Minneapolis to talk theater, he insisted that every play at the Guthrie would not be a centuries-old classic. He also believed in what he called "American Classics," and he listed such possible candidates for that honor as *Death of a Salesman*, *The Skin of Our Teeth*, and a bawdy bit of nonsense from the 1930's that Guthrie loved entitled, *Three Men on a Horse*.

The Guthrie theater has yet to do *Three Men on a Horse*, but they have dipped into American comedy classics, in presenting *Merton of the Movies*, and *The Beauty Part*.

Guthrie moved on from Minneapolis after the first three seasons, but he returned as guest director until his death.

By the end of its eighth season in 1970, attendance at the Guthrie theater had hit a new low. The possible reasons for the lack of attendance made for dandy dinner table conversation all over town. Minneapolitans like to debate the Guthrie's problems as much as they like to worry out loud about the Vikings or the Twins.

There was one good sign for the future of the theater, however. Michael Langham, who had worked with Guthrie in England and Canada, was named artistic director of the company. Langham arrived in Minneapolis in time to give the 1970 season one big hit. He directed the first world production of *A Play* by Aleksandr Solzhenitsyn, the Soviet Russian writer who was named in 1970 to receive the Nobel Prize for Literature.

Nicollet Mall.

Langham's production received widespread critical praise and ended an otherwise unfortunate season with a boom in attendance.

Audience attendance percentages have gone up and down during the theater's 10 years of operation, from an 84.2 per cent of theater capacity in 1963 to a high of 86.9 in 1968. The attendance low was in 1970 with 60.8 per cent of capacity.

In the 1971 season, Langham directed one of the theater's all-time hits, a revival of Edmond Rostand's play, "Cyrano de Bergerac." It was translated and adapted by Anthony Burgess and featured Paul Hecht in the title role. It played to 95.9 per cent of capacity.

Its success led Langham and Burgess to restage the play in a musical version, starring Christopher Plummer. The production spent its "try out" period in Minneapolis before touring to Broadway in 1973.

Langham's 1971 and 1972 seasons also saw the emergence as "stars" of such company members as Roberta Maxwell, Bernard Behrens and Peter Michael Goetz. Len Cariou, a company favorite who divided his time between acting classic roles in Minneapolis and starring in hit musicals on Broadway, made his debut as a Guthrie director in 1972. His production of John Steinbeck's play, "Of Mice and Men," was well-received by audiences and critics.

During the 1973 season, actress June Havoc—who had, as a child, appeared in vaudeville in Minneapolis with her sister, the late Gypsy Rose Lee—returned in a new role. She is the writer of the play, "I, Said the Fly," which had its world premiere at the Guthrie Theater.

The Guthrie theater and its resident repertory company are too much a part of the Minneapolis cultural scene now to fade away. Minneapolitans, if they remain true to their tradition, won't let that happen.

There is no doubt that it was because of the Guthrie that Minneapolis was rediscovered by the entertainment world.

Director Gower Champion and actress Mary Martin returned to the Orpheum Theater on downtown Hennepin Avenue to rehearse and try out the road company of "Hello Dolly" that toured Vietnam.

Producer Ross Hunter filmed the snowy airport scenes for the movie, "Airport," at the Twin Cities International Airport. During that period, one could meet Helen Hayes shopping on the Nicollet Mall, Burt Lancaster jogging along Washington Avenue and the late Van Heflin swimming at the Minneapolis Athletic Club. The movie also gave thousands of Twin Citizens a chance to see themselves on screen as "extras" in the crowd scenes. When the film was released, it played to packed houses for nine months in Minneapolis.

Hunter's success turned the Twin Cities into a little bit of Hollywood-on-the-Mississippi. Scenes for three major films, "Slaughterhouse Five," "The Heartbreak Kid," and "The Emigrants," were photographed in the area. The activity spawned a flurry of independent, locally-produced movies aimed at the national market. And the backgrounds for the Mary Tyler Moore television show also show off Minneapolis.

The fact that Hunter picked Minneapolis as a location for *Airport* because he needed a cold and blustery snowscape leads to another bit of theatrical trivia. For years, Minneapolis was known as the "home of frozen shows." Two of the major ice shows started here.

Eddie and Roy Shipstad and their friend, the late Oscar Johnson, put together their first Shipstads and Johnson *Ice Follies* at the old Minneapolis Arena. A few years later, Morris Chalfen, produced *Holiday on Ice*, an extravaganza that has toured to almost every corner of the world.

Chalfen, who continues to live in his hometown, is a modest man who is better known to more people in Moscow than in Minneapolis. The Russian friends he made during the many tours to the Soviet Union by the *Holiday on Ice* troupes gave Chalfen a chance to bring Russian dance groups and circuses to the United States.

I've said that Minneapolis audiences are eager. In most cases they are also devoted and good.

Again, in his book, *A New Theatre*, Tyrone Guthrie left Minneapolis audiences with a challenge. "It is our hope," he wrote, "that gradually, as audience and management become mutually better acquainted, the audience will begin to create the sort of theatre which it wants, which will be an expression of itself.

"Only thus can the intention of this project be fully realized. It is much more than merely building a theatre and creating a series of productions. The ultimate aim is to attract a creative audience."

That's a tough assignment from a top director. So far, the Minneapolis audience has tried enthusiastically to learn its role.

For the first time in Minneapolis' 100-plus years as a city, *some* of its residents wish that *all* of its boosters would pipe down.

These worried Minneapolitans suffer from a kind of reverse chauvinism. It has caused them to be overly protective of the city's bountiful way of life and to deplore the publicity it has received in recent years in such major magazines as *Time* and *Fortune*. They fear, of course, that if the Twin Cities attractions become too well-known, the area will suffer from all of the problems that urban growth can bring.

It is difficult, though, to hide a big city. It's even tougher when the city has an attractive twin. Together, Minneapolis and St. Paul have created a prairie metropolis that is too good to be ignored.

Business truly appreciates the local climate—economic and social if not physical—so much that it has turned the area into a "home office" capital.

Prosperous family-owned companies have expanded to international prominence by staying put in the Twin Cities. It is also interesting to note that often when a locally-owned firm has been sold to an outside buyer, the home office remained in the Twin Cities—particularly after the out-of-towner got to know the territory.

The list of major firms with home offices in the cities and suburbs is an impressive one. In Minneapolis, in addition to Dayton-

The city on the river side from the IDS Tower. The two low buildings to the left of the curving 3rd Ave. bridge belong to the post office (the larger of the two is the main post office). City hall is the building with the clock tower to the right of the picture. Note the parking lots toward the river. That is urban renewal land. Piece by piece, it is being built up. Note at the extreme left is the Yamasaki building, our Towers rising behind it (by the post office). That thing in foreground labeled NW is the Northwestern bank Weatherball—white, cold tonight; red, warm weather ahead; green, no change foreseen. And blinking means precipitation.

Almost the same view at night during the holiday season when buildings (before the fuel crisis) are illuminated with strings of lights.

I described the fish houses as our contribution to architectural history. Here are some on Lake Minnetonka, 20 minutes from downtown Minneapolis.

Hudson, General Mills, Honeywell, IDS and Pillsbury, the list includes Apache, Bemis, Cargill, Control Data, Fingerhut, Gamble-Skogmo, Gold Bond, Green Giant, S. J. Groves, International Multifoods, Northrup King, Peavey, Tennant, Tonka and Toro.

Twin City Federal Savings & Loan in Minneapolis is the largest of its kind in 49 states. Only one California firm can top it.

The two largest bank holding companies in the United States are Minneapolis-based and so are two major airlines—North Central and Northwest Orient. (Their home airport in Minneapolis, also known as Wold-Chamberlain Field, once served the small airplanes of Charles A. Lindbergh of Little Falls, Minn. Lindbergh, after his famous transatlantic flight in 1927, returned to his Minnesota home to fly his Congressman father around the state on campaign trips).

Prudential Insurance built its midwest home office on the shore of a Minneapolis lake. Two other major insurance firms, Lutheran Brotherhood and Northwestern National Life created their own gardens in downtown Minneapolis.

The Rev. Billy Graham's world headquarters overlooks Loring Park in downtown Minneapolis. Dr. Graham, who is a frequent Minneapolis visitor, began his Youth for Christ crusades while serving as president of a Minneapolis Bible college. And two other major religious denominations have world headquarters in Minneapolis and suburbs—the American Lutheran Church and the Evangelical Free Church of America.

Minneapolis has also had a long history of providing a friendly climate for medical research and good health care. Even so, it is not as well known a medical center as Rochester, Minn., a smaller city about an hour's drive south.

Open heart surgery was pioneered by a team of doctors at the University of Minnesota Hospitals and School of Medicine. Dr. Christiaan Barnard, the headline-making South African surgeon, trained at University Hospitals.

University researchers helped to develop the Salk polio vaccine. It is of some historical interest that Minneapolis also provided a haven to Sister Elizabeth Kenny. Before World War II, the Australian nurse was a controversial figure in the medical profession because of her method of treating polio. The Kenny Institute which Sister Kenny founded with Minneapolis help continues to treat patients suffering from other crippling diseases.

One of the best teaching hospitals in the United States is Hennepin County General Hospital in downtown Minneapolis. Positions on its staff are sought after by young medical students. Many doctors stay in Minneapolis to practice medicine after completing their internships and residencies at General.

Minneapolis provided a background setting for novelist Sinclair Lewis, who lived in its Kenwood District off and on, and for Max Shulman, who attended the University. Robert Penn Warren, Saul Bellow, Harry Reasoner, Eric Severeid, Mary McCarthy, and Allen Tate also did some writing in Minneapolis while living there or teaching there or both. The award-winning poet, John Berryman, while on the faculty at the University, leaped to his death from a bridge over the Mississippi River.

Certainly the University's presence drew many of these writers to Minneapolis and St. Paul, but the Twin Cities also serves as a publishing center. Major publishers of law books, astrological magazines and books, religious books and Bibles, including Dr. Billy Graham's "Decision" magazine, and agricultural publications, including "The Farmer" magazine, are in the metropolitan area.

The Ridder family, publishers of the St. Paul Pioneer Press and Dispatch newspapers, own newspapers across the United States. The Minneapolis Star and Tribune Company, headed by John Cowles Jr., owns *Harper's* magazine and is a stockholder in the New York publishing firm of Harper and Row.

In the 1950s—100 years after it was chartered as a city—Minneapolis made some mistakes. Fortunately, it didn't destroy itself as so many big cities did. For that, its residents can thank a few creative-thinking men representing business, labor and politics. Together, they went to work to sell the idea of an inner-city renaissance.

Minneapolis lost private homes and acres of park land to the freeway builders before second thoughts put a stop to it. The Minneapolis park board, in fact, fought the highway builders to the U.S. Supreme Court in an effort to block a freeway through historic Minnehaha Park. They lost the lawsuit, but freeway plans were changed as a result of the campaign.

Urban redevelopment enhanced downtown Minneapolis, but the city lost at least one major architecturally noteworthy building because of it. The furor over the destruction of the Metropolitan building laid the groundwork for the creation of the Minneapolis Heritage Preservation Commission, an official body which now has jurisdiction over all historic structures in the city.

The Nicollet Mall led to the organization of the Committee on Urban Environment (CUE) by former Mayor Arthur Naftalin. The CUE committee includes expert designers and planners who serve as volunteers to advise the city council on urban design problems. The committee's CUE awards each year are given to individuals, business and industry and organizations that have worked to improve the city.

Minneapolis takes pride in its extensive building program that provided its elderly with individually-designed new housing. The housing was planned by the Minneapolis Housing and Redevelopment Authority (HRA). The HRA also promoted a different approach to urban renewal in which old structures are rehabilitated rather than razed. Purpose of the program is to restore aging city neighborhoods.

The renovation of inner city residential areas by private enterprise has also been pushed by energetic community organizations of neighborhood residents. The groups of taxpayers and tenants are well-organized, visible and often very vocal at public meetings about civic plans.

As Minneapolis points toward the 21st century, two problems top a long civic list of "things that need doing." One is housing and the other is public transit.

Returnees from the suburbs have moved back inside the city limits to reclaim and restore certain neighborhoods that had been neglected. The renewed interest in preservation and restoration will continue the Minneapolis trend toward city revitalization.

More housing, however, will be needed. Present plans call for new apartments and townhouses downtown at the end of the Nicollet Mall near Loring Park and along the riverfront.

Public transit—something other than the present bus system or in addition to it—is being debated by all of the governmental agencies involved in metropolitan planning.

Under consideration are automated transit ways underground and above ground including a controversial "people mover" system attached to buildings in the Minneapolis business district. To get to St. Paul and around the suburban areas, Minneapolis' principal planner prefers an underground subway.

It is obvious that helter-skelter freeway-building has stopped in both cities due to public opinion about the noise, dirt and blight freeways bring to neighborhoods.

City officials also realized that more freeways added to the automobile population. Minneapolis has planned a series of parking ramps at the edge of the business district and has hopes of ridding itself of the ugly open parking lots sometime in the future. While plans proceed, some city officials are discussing ideas to set beautification standards for the parking lots.

Two aldermen have asked city planners to design commuter bike paths along important city streets to encourage city dwellers to bike downtown in an atmosphere safe from cars.

* * *

When Leslie Park, retired Minneapolis real estate executive, first proposed a second-story skyway between two buildings back in 1953, a lot of people laughed. Then, when Donald C. Dayton pushed for the Nicollet Mall on the city's main shopping street, there was more laughter.

It wasn't too loud, though, because Park's first skyway was already up. As for the Mall, a six-year-success-story in downtown retailing, it is scheduled to grow several blocks longer.

Some people, brainstorming on how to cope with Minneapolis winters, have talked about a dome over downtown or the entire inner city. Such a dome would allow zestful residents to bicycle in shirtsleeves all year around. It might also strengthen the current trend to take the city away from the motorist and give it back to the pedestrian.

Call it too idealistic or even idiotic, but it's not impossible. The next generation of Minneapolitans is getting ready right now to keep up the traditional and often incredible civic spirit. Just give them and us, 27 more years.

Then, why not plan to enjoy the next turn-of-the-century under glass in remarkable Minneapolis?